Praise for *On*

This book isn't theoretical. It's not fi... ...with ...ity and insight. It's a clear and compelling call to con... ...nat it means to be the people of God in the midst of a severely broken and battered world. Doug Logan is a practitioner and a theologian, a helpful guide.

MATT CHANDLER
Lead Pastor, The Village Church

In the tradition of Jesus and Paul, Pastor Doug Logan falls in the category of, "Don't know how to label him." He can be found one day in a robe preaching at a Presbyterian church, and the next out "on the block" in Camden conversing with the homies. He incarnates a robust orthodoxy with a well-worn orthopraxy, all of which bleeds through the pages of this book. I hope this is one of just many more offerings to come from his hand.

BRYAN LORITTS
Lead Pastor, Abundant Life
Author, *Saving the Saved*

What an insightful and helpful book! *On the Block* brims with integrity, authenticity, practicality, and hope because Doug Logan is not first a church theoretician; he is first a pastor in one of America's most broken cities. As I read, I was lovingly provoked, rebuked, and challenged, and you will be too. This is a book for such a time as this, written by a man who lives the missional gospel he writes about. If you're a pastor, this book may just change some of your fundamental assumptions about the ministry to which you've been called. Read *On the Block* and then go out and live it. You'll be glad you did.

PAUL TRIPP
President, Paul Tripp Ministries
Author of *Dangerous Calling*

Sentness is not simply a suggestion for something we should do but a command that shapes the way we are called to live. Doug, in a simple yet compelling way, paints a powerful portrait of what a sent life looks like on your city block or neighborhood cul-de-sac.

CHAN KILGORE
Lead Pastor, CrossPointe Church, Orlando
Acts 29 Florida Regional Director

On the Block is theology meets missiology meets practicality. It is Jesus on the streets from a street smart and real life guy who, while he could give you a missiological treatise on the gospel, instead shows you through precept *and* everyday living what it looks like to live on mission for Jesus individually and as a church.

TOMMY KIEDIS
Senior Pastor, Spanish River Church, Boca Raton, FL

On the Block is a challenging call to join God in responding to the needs of our communities. Doug Logan shares not only a strong biblical reason, but many heartwarming as well as heartbreaking stories of ministering in a difficult city. This is a book that not only every church planter should read, but anyone serving to bring the gospel to a lost world.

RON TOBIAS
Director of Church Planting Ministry, Spanish River Church, Boca Raton, FL

On the Block is a call to a ministry of action not just words. Doug Logan contextualizes in a very meaningful and pragmatic presentation how to carry out urban ministry through gospel eyes.

VICTOR D. FIGUEROA
Executive Director of the Housing Authority of the City of Camden

Pastor Logan's adaptability principles for success in urban ministry are built upon a *sentness* responsibility that requires us all as Christians to seek God's called people all the days of our lives. Like Pastor Logan I am a Christian and I am not unfamiliar with or scared of the urban context; I grew up in Camden and have chosen to work there, but this reminder of my *sentness* obligation as an active participant in the change of this city makes me uncomfortable. Thank you Pastor Logan for turning my focus to "missional engagement" as "a core component of Christian identity."

MANNY DELGADO
Former Executive Director of the Cramer Hill Community Development Corporation; Chief Operations Officer / Lead Person at Leap Academy University Charter School

ON THE BLOCK

DEVELOPING A BIBLICAL PICTURE
FOR MISSIONAL ENGAGEMENT

DOUG LOGAN

MOODY PUBLISHERS
CHICAGO

Edited by Linda Joy Neufeld
Interior and Cover design: Erik M. Peterson
Cover image: copyright © 2015 by Bernardojbp / iStock (61664176). All rights reserved.
Author photo: Avery Q. Logan

Library of Congress Cataloging-in-Publication Data
Names: Logan, Doug, author.
Title: On the block : developing a biblical picture for missional engagement
  / Doug Logan.
Description: Chicago : Moody Publishers, 2016. | Includes bibliographical
  references.
Identifiers: LCCN 2016029566 (print) | LCCN 2016032637 (ebook) | ISBN
  9780802414724 | ISBN 9780802414724 ()
Subjects: LCSH: Witness bearing (Christianity) | Evangelistic work. |
  Missions.
Classification: LCC BV4520 .L555 2016 (print) | LCC BV4520 (ebook) | DDC
  269/.2--dc23
LC record available at https://lccn.loc.gov/2016029566

We hope you enjoy this book from Moody Publishers. Our goal is to provide high-quality, thought-provoking books and products that connect truth to your real needs and challenges. For more information on other books and products written and produced from a biblical perspective, go to www.moodypublishers.com or write to:

Moody Publishers
820 N. LaSalle Boulevard
Chicago, IL 60610

1 3 5 7 9 10 8 6 4 2

Printed in the United States of America

This book is dedicated to the loving memory of my beautiful, Christ loving Mother, who is lavishly enjoying the permanent presence of Jesus in heaven. Through trials, test, and sickness you always showed me Jesus was life now and life eternal.

Charm is deceptive, and beauty does not last; but a woman who fears the Lord will be greatly praised.

PROVERBS 31:30

To my wife Angel, and my sons: Bernie, Aharon, and Avery, I love you so much and words can't express the joy I get in being husband, father, and pastor in our family. This book does not happen without your love, support, prayers, and encouragement.

CONTENTS

FOREWORD

Those who know me are aware of my passion for urban ministry. No matter what I'm doing it sort of comes out of me. Although I grew up in a harsh urban environment, my passion doesn't come from there, but from the might of the gospel to change all things for maximum use for our great God. We are in an age of urbanization, in which there is a resurgence of interest in the city. In general you have the expansion of urban renewal through gentrification, urban college expansion, small and large business expansion, art hubs, as well as hubs for connoisseur concentrations of all types. With all of the renewal going on there are the old urban issues: drugs, crime, racism, classism, socioeconomic brokenness, poverty, redlining, housing limitations, the breakdown of the family, fatherlessness, and much more.

Amid these is the need from comprehensive gospel renewal. The need for gospel renewal is greater than it was after the northern migration. Now urban has taken not only the form of a culture concentrated in large cities, but in smaller concentrated cities like Camden, Trenton, and Paterson in New Jersey, Flint and Grand Rapids in Michigan, Wilmington in Delaware, and

Coatesville in Pennsylvania. I applaud the works of the urban missiologists who wrote during the nineteenth century, but there needs to be a massive surge of indigenously urban scholarly practitioners who write of out of both study and street cred.

That is why this work by one of my sons in the ministry—friend and fellow elder Doug Logan—is so timely. In watching Doug for over a decade, it wows me how the Spirit works in and through him on the front lines of gospel ministry. *On the Block* is a needed work in the landscape of growing interest and ministry in urban inner cities. Doug does a great job rooting his work in the Bible and history, yet making it clear that it isn't merely studied in the tower, but strived for on the block. It is hard to read this book and not feel convicted about one's commitment to incarnational evangelism.

Because Doug is a pastor, he sees the need for incarnational engagement to go beyond being centered on one hyper-gifted person, but something that the whole church must be committed to and viewed as a lifestyle by all. As you read story after story of real people who experience conversion and transformation beyond the altar call, you see long-lasting and life-lifting conversions that turn into multiplying the work of the kingdom. Doug moves inner-city ministry beyond toxic charity, paternalism, messiah complexes, and cheap grace, to a place that echoes the word of the Lord to Paul, "Do not be afraid, but go on speaking and do not be silent, for I am with you, and no one will attack you to harm you, for I have many in this city who are my people" (Acts 18:9–10). It is clear that he is fearless in his commitment, yet biblically stout in his understanding, to engaging some of the most difficult corners of urbana.

Everyone inside and outside of the urban context will benefit holistically from the biblical grid and wealth of practical knowledge. In addition, this should be a go-to resource for those who are seeking a rich introduction to urban ministry. Read this work and see the front lines in a fresh and refreshing way that will help you to be and mobilize others for effective front-line gospel ministry.

DR. ERIC MASON
Founder and Senior Pastor, Epiphany Fellowship, Philadelphia

PROLOGUE

The theological underpinning of my approach to missions can be summed up in a single sentence: *I believe that we must simultaneously promote the importance of the church in missions (ecclesiology) and the importance of missions in the church (missiology), while looking to Christ (Christology) as our model.*

In other words, we cannot set a sharp distinction between church and missions. Growing up in an urban Baptist church, this was a dichotomy I grew accustomed to. I was raised with two false, embarrassingly oversimplified illustrations of ministry styles.

The first was a wandering evangelization whose sole focus was on pushing folks toward salvation. It followed Jesus' ministry example as it spread the gospel through scattering seeds as far and wide as possible. But it didn't linger to encourage and foster growth—which Jesus also did! The goal was simply to have as many people as possible hear the basic contours of the gospel message, staying just long enough to prompt salvation prayers before moving on to the next stop.

The other saw as its goal to explain abstract theology while berating a static faith community. It looked to Paul as it spread seeds over a very narrow area, and remained there in perpetuity. The goal was focused on the growth and full maturity of the people sitting in the pews each Sunday. The gospel is preached within the four walls of the church, but remains static, not moving out into the community. Evangelization only occurred in the specific arena of the church, or not at all.

I've met many who followed one or the other of these extremes. But you cannot pit them against each other. Isolated, they are both incorrect. Missions without a strong foundation in the church creates wandering believers who roam outside of communities. As a result, their faith rarely reaches maturity and produces weakness of conviction. Although many will hear the gospel, and a good number might verbally commit to the faith, this method of missions fails to provide the sort of all-encompassing nourishment of the Christian walk. At worst, it leaves fledgling faiths susceptible to being choked out by weeds, scorched by the sun, or eaten by birds.

Conversely, those who keep the church separate and distinct from missional engagement stifle the gospel. Such thinking fails to catch the urgency of God's calling to all believers to spread His Word. Entire flocks of Christians come to feel as though "missions" is something for those unassociated with the church—it is simply for those missionaries "on the front lines." Missions is conceived as something to which the church donates money, not something it actually engages in. Thus, the tools of the Holy Spirit grow rusty, held back by an inert missional culture.

The starting point for a biblically informed and Christ-honoring urban mission is a third way that brings these two extremes together. We must shepherd and disciple our congregation while instilling within them a relentless drive to move the gospel *outward* into the surrounding community. We see in the ministries of Jesus and Paul a strong emphasis on personal spiritual growth, good teaching, gospel proclamation, and outward-focused action. Our Christology drives us to be *missiological* ecclesiologists and *ecclesiological* missiologists.

When we live out the gospel within community in a hostile world, we become authentically reformed. If the hostile world is removed, that's not reformed theology—that's comfy-couch religion.

For me, what's missing in the hood is hope and family. So that's the cultural context I seek to create. I want to speak hope into their hopelessness, and I want to create family where there is none. So that's why they're invited into my house. That's why I crack jokes. This arena is the grace-turning-of-the-soil that seems to be very ripe for people to come to saving knowledge of Christ and for churched people to come to the reality that they're not saved. That's my goal: that people would see Jesus high and lifted up, and know of His majesty. And so in missional living, we make that clear. In missional living, we seek to create an atmosphere of hope in an environment of grace. Not just for this generation, but also for the next.

On the block, many believe no one cares about them, let alone their children, or their grandchildren. We want men and women and their children and their grandchildren to know they are cared for, and then be consumed and immersed in the grace

> **In missional living, we seek to create an atmosphere of hope in an environment of grace.**

of Jesus. We want multigenerational impact so that even our grandchildren are laced in the gospel, grow up in it, smell it, go to college with it, have life with it, and let it surround their every decision. That's how we will have generational impact. That's the ultimate way to fight racism and to fight classism. It's through the gospel. We have to leave a legacy of grace. And a legacy of grace is not about you. It's about the grace of God being the subject of the story, not you. You're just the tagline. The grace of God has to be the source of our generational legacy.

PART 1

FOUNDATIONS

"God loves to be depended on. So He gives imperfect, inadequate human beings impossible assignments."[1]

CRAWFORD LORITTS

CHAPTER 1

ADAM

My first years in the ministry were trying times for me spiritually. I struggled to understand the importance of a comprehensive picture of missional engagement. I believe this was due in part to my failure to fully understand the biblical framework of missional engagement. As I got older and was discipled, I began to learn that the entire Bible was God's missional plan to redeem lost humanity. As I turned to the Scriptures, the centrality of this component to missional engagement suddenly leapt off of the page. Everything changed in how I engaged the block when I understood Genesis 3 in light of the mission of God.

Missions began in Genesis 3 when Adam and Eve disobeyed God's command. Adam and his wife ate of the one fruit that God forbade them to eat, and in that began the cataclysmic fall of all mankind that would come after them. What a tragedy! The picture here is Adam having full reign of the King's garden, an overabundance of food provided by God, and yet stealing from the tree he was not permitted to eat from. In this definitive act of disobedience Adam commits high treason against the King—an act punishable by death for him and all his offspring.

At this very moment in history, Adam is in need of a Redeemer. In the midst of Adam's sin, God initiates contact with him. It is important to notice that after Adam sins against God, he doesn't come running to God in confession, but God comes to Adam. God sets a plan in place for his redemption. Even in pronouncing judgment and the curse, God graciously provides redemption in His promise to bring forth a Messiah. God announces the plan to the serpent in Genesis 3:14–15:

> So the LORD God said to the serpent, "Because you have done this, "Cursed are you above all livestock and all wild animals! You will crawl on your belly and you will eat dust all the days of your life. And I will put enmity between you and the woman, and between your offspring and hers; he will crush your head and you will strike his heel."

This proclamation is what is called the protoevangelium, meaning the first (*proto*) message of salvation (*evangelium*). Genesis 3:15 was the first promise to Adam that God would send a Messiah and save His people. Instead of destroying him, God has made a way for man to be restored through God's means. The means was that God would raise up His own Son to be a sacrifice. Jesus, the Son of God, would be a propitiation for man's sin and rebellion. It would be imbedded in His nature—in His very DNA.

The head of the serpent would be crushed. We know that it could not be accomplished by any like Adam who have been subjected to sin. It would take someone blameless and fully righteous before God to conquer Satan. God tells Adam that such a man would come—and indeed He did come: Christ, fully man and fully God. Jesus, the Son of God, would crush the head of the serpent!

In this passage from Genesis 3, God is the one who first reaches out to Adam. God is the first apostle, sent of His own initiation, to save His people. God is the first Missionary to step into man's problems and offer His peace and presence. God is the first Evangelist. He engages Adam missionally, first with a clear decree of his downfall and destruction based on his sin, and second with a promise that an offspring would come who would right this wrong.

We must remember that when we express the gospel, we are merely repeating the words of our Lord. We are mirroring His proactive engagement with the gospel, which began as soon as man fell. God didn't waste time: man sinned and God sent a message of redemption.

God sent Himself to engage sinful man. Therefore, we must also follow the call to go to the lost people on the block. Based on God's example to us, our missional engagement must be an active, intentional engagement with the world. The world that is in need of the message of hope, the gospel, and the man of hope, Jesus! This message of hope can't just be relegated to a chosen group of people (insiders), but mainly people outside of Christ. I like to call this living "sent-lives." The church must understand its *sentness*, and how *sentness* flows from and out of the implications of the Great Commission. As we seek to obey and apply the work of the Great Commission, we find that every Christ follower is commanded in Scripture to a life of being a missionary who initiates contact with the lost world. This is what God did in the garden, and this is what we must do in our cities.

CHAPTER 2

NEHEMIAH

Put simply: the book of Nehemiah is a snapshot of the biblical reality that people need to be restored before the city can be rebuilt. It is a construction plan to rebuild the brokenness of the whole city—its people, families, property, and government structures. Nehemiah recognized through God's direction that the people themselves had to be changed first before Jerusalem could be fixed. If we want to rebuild our cities, then we need to heed Nehemiah's example. A city without transformed people will eventually come crumbling down. Nehemiah's work foreshadows Christ's work of transforming hearts so that changed people can be used to rebuild the surrounding world.

The book of Nehemiah takes place after the Babylonians attacked the Israelites and destroyed the wall that enclosed Jerusalem. This humiliating defeat made God's people incredibly vulnerable; Proverbs 25:28 uses the image of an unwalled city to suggest utter ruin. The Babylonians—an idol-worshiping army—had entered Jerusalem and its holy temple, torn down its fortifications, burned the gates, and hauled many of God's own people into exile and slavery. Life in Jerusalem was no longer secure.

The book of Lamentations tells us that God's people were devastated and God's name was disgraced among the surrounding countries. Brokenness became the status quo for 141 years. God's people could not worship together, and the handful who remained lived in shame and poverty. The situation seemed hopeless. It starts with Nehemiah hearing about Jerusalem's devastation. He was living in the Persian capital city as a high-ranking servant of the king. His job as cupbearer to the king meant that he sampled the monarch's drink and food to check for poison (perhaps the closest modern equivalent is our Secret Service). Although Jerusalem had now been a devastated city for generations, God uses that meeting to radically transform Nehemiah's heart and life, and through him the state of the city.

> **A city without transformed people will eventually come crumbling down.**

NEHEMIAH SAW THE HURT

Nehemiah saw the brokenness of his city and his people, and it caused him to weep, fast, and pray for three or four months. He realized that the fractured state of everything was not the way it was supposed to be. As we live on city blocks, we encounter systems that are broken and devastated, but because things have been that way for a long time—almost 150 years in Nehemiah's case—it's easy to fall into the trap of thinking that this is normal; it's the way that things always have been and it's the way that they always will be.

Like Nehemiah, we need to grieve. Nehemiah's desire to

change his people's destitution began with an emotional change of heart. He asked with compassion about the condition of Jerusalem and his people and learned that the people were shamed, the buildings crumbling, and the city was wrecked. It used to be fly and now it was just a hot mess.

In cities across the globe there are buildings and areas in disrepair, ruined and dilapidated. Broken piles of bricks are still there, never cleared away or rebuilt. Are we content to simply sit at a distance as silent observers?

Nehemiah embraced his new perspective by launching into a prolonged season of prayer. He looked out at the conditions but did not find much reason for hope. We do the same in the cities we all serve across this country and the world. At the time this book was written, Jerusalem was already in ruins with no apparent remedy. A devastated city is ugly and depressing, but God is altogether lovely, worthy, and wonderful. In his grief, Nehemiah had to look to God as the source of his hope.

NEHEMIAH IN CONFESSION

Nehemiah stepped into the grief, pain, and hurt of Jerusalem's shame, and made a heartfelt confession to his God. He repented for his sin as well as the sin of his family and the sin of his city. He intentionally looked beyond himself into his block.

This is diametrically opposed to individualistic thinking, which focuses on self and independence without accountability to anyone else. Paul says in the New Testament that we are the church, and the church is like a body: if one part suffers, everyone suffers with it (1 Cor. 12:26). Remember what God has promised: if we return to Him, repent and walk in the Word by the power of His Spirit, He will live among us as our God and King.

Nehemiah didn't sit back and say, "You know, some bad people have really jacked up my church and my city. I'll tweet about them and post what they did on Facebook." Instead he owned the city's problems, essentially saying: "I've helped create this problem myself." He identified his own guilt and confessed his own sin.

NEHEMIAH LOOKS TO GOD FOR HOPE

Nehemiah had the realistic humility to see that he could never rebuild his city alone. He asked for the king's permission and blessing to gather a team that would rebuild Jerusalem, then gave up his position in the palace.

Knowing this endeavor would mean the end of all his other dreams, Nehemiah prepared to go back to the place he now desperately wanted to rebuild. He talked to Artaxerxes, the Persian king, a man who was opposed to the nation of Israel and held him captive. Nehemiah sought and found help in unlikely places! Artaxerxes personally permitted his trip and gave him the supplies and authority needed to reach and restore Jerusalem.

In doing this, Nehemiah is a shadow of Jesus' ministry of restoration. Both gave up a high position in order to identify with the plight of their people, both developed and fulfilled a specific mission, and both of their lives were characterized by prayerful dependence upon God.

Nehemiah gave up his cushy job as the cupbearer in the palace and risked his life going home to his hood, an unwalled city. He traded his health benefits and soft bed for a cot in a house that probably lacked a roof. He put his career, comfort, and life on the line to do what God was calling him to do. It's going to cost you something to follow Jesus in building up what has been broken down. The calling of God is not pretty and neat; it doesn't fit per-

fectly into our ideal denominational box. It is messy and dangerous: lives are at stake, there are housing and racial implications,
and it can often cost the inner-city missionary everything.

Nehemiah realized that he was not the only person still seeking after God and thanked the Lord that he wasn't the only one
moved by the Holy Ghost. I am under no illusion that the church
I serve is the only place God is working in my city. Furthermore,
I know that I am neither the only one who cares nor the only pastor whom God is using. However, I am honored to be a part of
what God is doing here.

NEHEMIAH BUILDS

Nehemiah assembled the families of Israel and began rebuilding the walls of Jerusalem piece by piece. Opposition assailed
the workers with fearsome rumors, scornful mockery, and death
threats. But these didn't faze Nehemiah; he told the workers to
have swords in one hand and hammers in the other. He stood
strong in the face of opposition because he trusted in God and had
a legacy in mind. We don't build up the broken cities for ourselves
but for our children, grandchildren, and great-grandchildren.
That is why we feed our family, teach children, support the police,
and pray at school ball games. Nehemiah looked beyond his own
comfort and security to the brokenness and danger of Jerusalem
for the sake of his people. It's not about us; it's for the present and
the future.

We want this city to be one of joy, just as Nehemiah did. He
wanted to help realize the promise of Jeremiah 33:9, where God
says: "This city shall be to me a name of joy, a praise and a glory
before all the nations of the earth who shall hear of all the good
that I do for them. They shall fear and tremble because of all the

good and all the prosperity I provide for it." This is the ultimate outcome of rebuilding work: God glorified, His name magnified, and the nations seeing and praising Him.

The collective work of Nehemiah concluded with a renewal of worship in the temple. There was a dedication of the reconstructed city walls, where the people sang praises and the priests taught the people the word of God (Neh. 12:27–30). Together they celebrated the wonderful works of God.

Prior to the project, the Israelites were a downtrodden people in a devastated city. God put together this fragmented community; though they weren't all builders, they sought to bless the city as a team and so accomplished things they never would have dreamed of doing. Our Lord has a long history of turning broken people into useful and beautiful vessels of His mercy. Paul, in a beautiful description, calls each believer Christ's workmanship or masterpiece (Eph. 2:10).

* * *

Nehemiah's motivating passion in his labor to rebuild Jerusalem was to make God famous among the nations of the earth. His example gives us hope today, as urban residents, that God has a heart for the city—even our city. Christianity has historically been an urban religion, reflecting the progression of the Bible's story: it begins in the garden of Eden but ends in a city, New Jerusalem.

One of my friends is a sculptor. When we would walk through the city of Philadelphia he'd almost always find shards of glass and rock or pieces of brick. He'd reach down, pick them off the ground and put them in his pocket. They seemed worthless to me—I thought he was crazy! Yet he would take those useless fragments from all over the city and form them into beautiful mosaics.

Nehemiah's rebuilding of the city of Jerusalem wasn't the real work; the people building up the city were God's masterpiece. The cement of that wall is gospel work. The gospel unifies us and makes us Christ's masterpiece. God takes people from all over the world—the broken, homeless, and fatherless—and glues us together into one family. Our family portrait then shows the world His majestic rebuilding project as we reach the least, the last, and the lost in the city.

CHAPTER 3

JESUS

If the gospel accounts teach us anything, it is that Jesus has an intense passion and love for people. His love and passion is most clearly displayed in His incarnation. Jesus left heaven, where He was continually worshiped by angels singing, "Holy, holy, holy," and tucked His *shekinah* glory away to put on a human suit so that He could physically dwell with us (John 1:14) and engage us with His loving grace. He ultimately gave up His life on Calvary's cross. Jesus gave up everything so He would be our everything!

The descent from perfect union within the Godhead to *take on human flesh*, from perfect light to utter darkness, from free and total dominion into a world of slavery, demonstrates His plain passion for people in His nature. He is literally the God-man, the Immanuel ("God *with* us").

Indeed the mere fact that the eternal Word came down to earth, became man, and "became flesh and dwelt among us" is the greatest act of intimate engagement one could possibly imagine. He came down to experience the same temptations to sin that we experience. He sought to fully empathize with our tribulations.

His passion for people is manifest not only in His nature, but in His ultimate purpose to serve as the propitiation for the sins of His people—a people hell-bent on disobeying Him. While all of humanity has turned against God and is plagued by mortal, self-inflicting wounds in our rebellion, Christ came, undeterred, to heal our suffering. This is a widespread healing that occurred through a one-time act of death and resurrection. This is a healing that is deeply personal, intimate. As He knows each hair on our head, He knows the stains that need to be washed away. Jesus entered into our mess and got His hands dirty. He pulled us out and cleaned us up with His grace in order that we might light up the world with His Word.

What's more, our Lord has not simply sought to be an empathetic Savior, but a personal *friend*. And while on earth, our Lord was fully emotionally engaged in the sufferings of others. He wept for the death of His friend Lazarus, despite knowing that He would soon resurrect him. He so intimately felt the pain of missing the earthly presence of this man that He *wept* with them.

Christ's ministry demonstrated closeness, even when He was surrounded by large groups of people. It is easy to misinterpret the instances when Christ fed the masses that followed Him, such as in Matthew 15. These scenes are not biblical versions of modern day soup kitchens—in which the hungry are fed but are not necessarily *cared for*. Christ provided for more than just the physical needs of His flock automatically at a scheduled time and place. This physical provision is an outward expression of a spiritual, eternal provision that is perfectly and personally calibrated to His flock's most ultimate need: namely, that of *Himself*.

The famous account of the woman at the well emphasizes the closeness of Jesus' ministry in another way by breaking through boundaries created by society. Here was a woman who had been an outcast, who had been branded by society as an immoral woman and thus not worthy of close relationships within the community. To be simply near to her was considered defiling. But Christ did not see her this way. He did not find her unworthy of His personal attention or unworthy of His touch. Instead, Christ had an altogether different vision of her. He saw her as she truly ought to be considered—as one who could receive grace and thus be adorned in righteousness. He saw her dining with Him in glory. Indeed He saw her in this light from the beginning of time.

What a vivid depiction of the contrast in vision between culture and Christ! Instead of allowing cultural categories to constrain His engagement, He saw her as a *suffering individual* who needed to be saved and elevated to the *highest* position known to man—an heir with Christ. Like the feeding of the masses, Christ's engagement was again personal, efficacious, and fully orbed.

This is the example that we must emulate. The church's missional engagement must be infused with true *compassion*. This is a compassion that, as we have seen, cares for the intimate and personal needs of people. It is a compassion that seeks to provide for *comprehensive* wholeness instead of a narrow conception of what we think a person needs. It is a compassion that rejects and eschews cultural constructions, hierarchies, and assumptions, when they keep us distant and cloud our capacity to use our holy imagination.

Jesus exemplified this quality of cultural sensitivity throughout the gospel accounts. He engages the woman with the issue of blood in Luke 8:43–48 ever so carefully, yet He made His salvation and her faith in Him the centerpiece of the conversation. Jesus was also very sympathetic without reducing His engagement into mere social justice with the demon-possessed man in

Mark 5:1–20. We watch Jesus subdue the evil agents of Satan. The man was in spiritual bondage and so physically strong that no one could hold him. Yet the power of El Elyon (the Strongest One) would step in and subdue the man, send the demons away, and set the man free. Immediately after that the man was ready to give his life to follow Jesus on mission, yet Jesus would command him to stay, as He states in Mark 5:19–20, "'Go home to your friends and tell them how much the Lord has done for you, and how he has had mercy on you.' And he went away and began to proclaim in the Decapolis how much Jesus had done for him, and everyone *marveled*" (emphasis added). Again, cultural sensitivity and the power of the gospel were at work.

I could bring up many more examples, but I would like to take your attention back to the woman at the well. Jesus is ever so gentle and yet potent with the truth of God's words. She is a Samaritan woman who has had multiple husbands, multiple divorces, and in light of the ancient Near-East culture she was every bit of a dreg to society and worthless in many ways based on her past. In that culture she would be listed amongst the least, last, and lost, particularly to a man and even more, to a man who was a Jewish rabbi.

The woman needed Jesus' saving power in the midst of her shame. I know a young man named Caleb who lived near my church building who tried everything to fix his life of heroin addiction. He struggled through multiple rehabilitation programs and centers, yet while he still struggled he still showed up to church. One day a pastor at my church shared the gospel with Caleb while he was high on drugs and very angry with the idea of God. Caleb received the Lord as Savior that day.

Caleb needed the power of the gospel in the midst of his

addiction. The dwellers on the block need the gospel. Jesus is the only "addiction" that satisfies. Jesus met the woman at the well in an unlikely place. Caleb met Jesus on the block, which for some is an unlikely place at an unlikely time. Caleb died young, only a few weeks after having received the Lord as Savior. We must have an uncompromised gospel engagement that is laced with cultural sensitivity and points to the Savior as the ultimate and immediate joy. Jesus is into meeting people at all kinds of places and times. Jesus meets people in their broken, godless, dead-in-sin conditions. He meets people on the block in their pain, their mess, their untimely situation, their thirst, their desperation, and in their baby daddy/momma drama.

Jesus was in a mess on the cross. A beautiful mess. On the cross, Jesus had pain, agony, and thirst. Yet in His perfect sensitivity, He took all the rejection and hatred but was sensitive to the lost He was drawing to Himself. "Father, forgive them, for they know not what they do" (Luke 23:34).

CHRIST COMMANDS *ALL* TO MISSIONAL ENGAGEMENT

Throughout the Gospels (as well as the beginning of Acts), Jesus provides both commands and descriptions of the roles of all His followers after His death and resurrection. They are both future job descriptions and job imperatives: what they will do is what they are commanded to do. Christ's command was not constrained to the select apostles for their particular task of founding the church. Rather, it is a universal command to all believers.

Jesus' *commissions* have received extensive treatment, but it is worth quickly revisiting three key passages. In John 20:21, Christ hints at the nature of the disciples' calling when He states, "As the Father sent me, even so I am sending you." In Acts 1:8 Christ gives His last exhortations to His apostles: "You will be my witnesses in Jerusalem and in all Judea and Samaria, and to the end of the earth." And most famously in Matthew 28:19–20, Christ gives what has since been called His Great Commission: "Go therefore and make disciples of all nations, baptizing them in the name of the Father and of the Son and of the Holy Spirit, teaching them to observe all that I have commanded you."

Although much more can be said about these passages, I will briefly highlight only three common characteristics of these verses: (1) they are global in aim and outward in direction, (2) they come as forward-looking commands, and (3) they are addressed to the church at large as those who are in covenant with Him.

These verses have a clear global and outward push to them. As new Christians, the disciples would have seen the world through a temple-centric lens. By God's command, God's people maintained separation from the nations for the sake of their own purity (Lev. 20:22–26). Israel was to be a blessing to the nations as the outsiders were called to the temple and were adopted into the covenant.

The outpouring of the Spirit at Pentecost brings radical transformation. Christ pushes His followers out from Jerusalem to take the gospel to purify the sinful nations (Acts 1:8). Purity is no longer maintained by excluding the unclean from the temple, but the living temple, Jesus Christ, comes to the unclean to purify them. This is seen most vividly when Jesus heals the leper and the women with the flow of blood. Jesus constantly did things that made Him unclean and seemingly disqualified to be God's Messiah. But Jesus Himself is the One who purifies. He makes His people clean by His touch of grace.

The command to go out would have challenged the disciples to go far and beyond the narrow strip of land in the Near East to reach the globe with the powerful, transforming good news of the Messiah. The Old Testament pictures the inclusion of the nations joining in the blessings of the people of God by joining with Israel on pilgrimage to the temple. In an unexpected twist, the temple goes on pilgrimage to the nations. The bricks that make up the New Testament temple are the people who have received Christ and have been transformed by the gospel.

The verbs Christ uses in each verse—"I am sending," "You will be . . . witnesses," and "go"—are all in the future imperative tense. They are not mere suggestions or helpful hints. They are commands from our Lord. Those who are sent by God are commanded to go. *Sentness* is not simply a special spiritual gift or unique characteristic of certain Christians, it is a condition of proper obedience for all Christians. We must take this calling seriously, but more on that later.

Although Christ was speaking directly to the disciples, His command is for the entire corporate body of the church—each and every one of its members. Not simply the pastors or missions teams, but all of us have been commanded and commissioned. All of us, as brothers and sisters in Christ, have been called and sent.

We see this explicitly in John 20:21, as Jesus sets Himself up as the model for missions. As He was sent by the Father, so are all believers sent. This is an essential part of what it means to be Christlike. Moreover, the word *witness* in Greek is the same as the word for *martyr*. Christ's command may have in view the entirety of Christian living, in which we die to ourselves and become alive in Christ. Missional living is a means by which we exhibit our lives as image bearers of Christ.

Thus, the sending of Jesus by the Father has far-reaching implications for our understanding of Christian sentness. All believers are recipients of the Spirit of God and have the same spirit of sentness that Christ had; therefore, all have responsibility and obligation to missional service. As missional living was an essential aspect of Christ's ministry, so should it be exhibited in the believer who strains to become more and more like the one by whose mission he was saved. It is, in other words, truly *every man and woman* who is called.

CHAPTER 4

PAUL

"And he gave the apostles, the prophets, the evangelists, the shepherds and teachers, to equip the saints for the work of ministry, for building up the body of Christ." (Ephesians 4:11–13)

The book of Acts picks up where Luke's gospel leaves off. We find Jesus continuing, by the aid of His Holy Spirit, to work in and through the apostles to see many and any come to know Him. The gospel has taken them from town to town and city to city. The physician Luke says that Christ followers must be on mission to reach the lost with the gospel of Christ. This mission would be a local, regional, and global one that would take them from Judea to Samaria and to the ends of the earth.

Acts 1:1 says, "I have dealt with all that Jesus began to do and teach." Luke's statement here carries the inference that we (the church today) are the continuation of what Jesus *began* in doing and teaching. I myself am an Acts 29 church planter, and for some, that's alarming. When I tell my African American family members who are primarily traditional African American Baptist and Pentecostal, they say it must be a cult because there are only twenty-eight chapters of Acts. The network is called Acts 29 as it is a play on the idea that the church is to continue the work of church planting now and until Christ returns.

We deeply believe that we are a part of the continuation of what Jesus began to do and teach in the book of Acts. Steve Childers puts it like this in his exhaustive manual on church planting, "The good news is that the radical, renewing work of God manifested in Jesus Christ in the first century, is continuing today by God's Holy Spirit through His Church. This is why the Church is the hope of the world."[2]

Paul's mission seemed to be fleshed out in a massive, robust church planting movement throughout Asia Minor and all of Europe—this was the known world at that time. Paul and his apostolic delegates had a deep sense of sentness.

When Paul opened his letter to his son in the faith, Titus, Paul identifies himself in the context of sentness. He says, "Paul, a servant of God and an apostle of Jesus Christ…" (Titus 1:1). He sees himself as a servant of God and is bound to serve Him with his whole life. The word *servant* (*doulos* in the Greek) has the connotation of one who is in a relationship of permanent servitude to another. Yet even deeper, the word implies a slave, one who is bound to another and is altogether consumed by the desires and will of another.

Paul then calls himself an apostle—or one sent forth. The sender would commission the apostle to go wherever he commanded. And that apostle would be sent with authority, be bound to the purpose of serving, and be completely consumed by the desires and will of the sender. The embodiment of this reality is a word I have been calling *sentness*.

Following the example of Christ, the apostles commanded their fellow believers to missional engagement. Paul, in his letter to Timothy, delivers his evangelizing encouragement in the form of commands that apply to the whole of the church. Paul writes,

> Until I come, devote yourself to the public reading of Scripture, to exhortation, to teaching. Do not neglect the gift you have, which was given you by prophecy when the council of elders laid their hands on you. Practice these things, immerse yourself in them, so that all may see your progress. Keep a close watch on yourself and on the teaching. Persist in this, for by so doing you will save both yourself and your hearers. (1 Timothy 4:13–16)

Do you sense the dogmatic drive to pursue evangelization in Paul's words? "Practice," "keep a close watch," and "persist" are the verbs he chooses. They show that this type of life must be fully engaged, ever vigilant, and fully consumed by the gospel.

Although Paul's commands are immediately directed toward Timothy, it must be remembered that these are commands for all believers. For Paul, to engage in missional living is to fulfill one's role as a minister of the faith. He did not leave evangelism in the context of a flighty idea or a whimsical sense of purpose. He did not say, "If you're called to be an evangelist, do the work." He did not say, "If the Spirit moves you and you feel the sense and purpose to evangelize, you should do it." He said, "*Do* the work," as a concise imperative. Indeed, not engaging in this gospel work would be *sin*.

It is important to note how thoroughly missional Paul's own life was as he diligently and faithfully did the work of an evangelist after meeting Christ on the road to Damascus. He planted churches in Lystra, Iconium, Derby, Philippi, and Thessalonica.

He met Lydia at a river in Philippi and started a church in her house. He was motivated to take ownership of and combat the darkness of the world around him, engaging the least, the last, and the lost with the gospel. His motivation for this life of missions was his identity in Christ: that he had been reconciled to God and had been brought into right relationship with Him.

The transformation Paul experienced as he encountered Jesus on the road to Damascus was the basis of his evangelical content. But more importantly for our purposes, his transformation was also the *impetus* for his missional engagement. As one who had been called to Christ, he was motivated by the notion that he had been sent to proclaim. He mirrored Christ not only by engaging in good works but by mirroring Christ's ministry itself! As he told the Galatians, "I have been crucified with Christ. It is no longer I who live, but Christ who lives in me. And the life I now live in the flesh I live by faith in the Son of God, who loved me and gave himself for me" (Galatians 2:20).

The explicit tie between missional engagement and our status as Christians is also made by the apostle Peter in 1 Peter 2:9, where he notes that the church is "a chosen race, a royal priesthood, a holy nation, a people for his own possession, *that you may proclaim the excellencies of him who called you out of darkness into his marvelous light*" (emphasis added). Note the close connection Peter makes between our status as those who are in covenant with Christ, who bear His image, and the outward expression of that status through evangelism—it is one of the *purposes* of our status as Christians that we engage in missions!

Not only does Paul echo Jesus' call to go, but he also follows Jesus' example of loving the lost. Luke writes for us a dossier of the apostle Paul's missionary journey in the book of Acts. It was almost like multiple Facebook posts by Paul, as he engaged each city with the gospel. Paul was on an overarching journey that would eventually take him to Athens in Greece.

Everyone knew about Athens; it was the foremost Greek city-state from the fifth century B.C. It was thick in philosophical tradition with brilliant scholars such as Socrates, Plato, and Aristotle. Paul found himself in Athens, the cultural and intellectual capital of the world. There were numerous temples, statues, shrines, and altars dedicated to the Greek gods and goddesses; in the Parthenon stood a huge golden statue (idol) of the Greek goddess Athena. There were images of the Greek god Apollo, and the city's patrons: Zeus, Poseidon, and Artemis—the entire Greek pantheon. All the ancient gods of Mt. Olympus were represented, and from an artistic perspective, they were awe-inspiring and beautiful, made of stone and glass, gold and silver, ivory and marble, assembled with meticulous, artistic precision. Paul was not impressed by this, nor was he overwhelmed. He was, rather, *underwhelmed* by the fact that there was no honor for the God and Father of the Lord Jesus Christ. This was a city submerged in its idols, and yet lost. "While Paul was waiting for them in Athens, he was greatly distressed to see that the city was full of idols" (Acts 17:16 NIV).

As Paul went through the city, he felt the weight of the godlessness there, and this roused him to mission, to see Jesus' name lifted high and made famous. The weight of the godlessness *grieved* his soul. What about us? Might the weight of the lostness of our own cities grieve *our* souls, and might God grant us a holy provocation to proclaim His name in our city? After all, we have just as many if not more idols in today's world. They just have different names.

Historians believe that the type of idolatry the apostle Paul witnessed in Athens was an elaborate picture of how ancient idols were worshiped. They were on high display as the centerpiece of the city, much like Times Square in New York City lights up during the New Years season. Note the word "provoked" means not just stirred and aroused with anger; the text isn't referring merely to the quality of Paul's emotional state. The translation above also brings out the missional *action* that was stirred from the grief and anger Paul experienced. He was provoked to proclaim Christ's name.

Paul saw the absence of Christ in the city. It provoked and roused him to anger and action. Amidst the high-brow architecture and rich history of the city Paul recognized that there was an absence of the worship of Jesus Christ, and that Jesus was not the centerpiece of life in that city. This should *always* tick us off! Not in such a way as to want to punch a hole in the wall, but to spark us toward missional *action*. He was annoyed, then aroused. Paul was annoyed by the idols, then aroused to mission.

An urban visionary has to see what isn't there.

Paul saw beyond the visual decadence of Athens. He saw what wasn't visibly apparent and he therefore was an urban visionary. An urban visionary has to see what isn't there. We have to see through *gospel eyes*; we must interpret through the lens of Scripture what God wants there.

Paul saw where there was no worship of Jesus, and even the greatest of cities in his day had foolishly turned to worship a pantheon of gods—culminating in ungodliness and godlessness altogether. In seeing the absence of worship to Jesus the Christ,

I believe he recognized that there were a bunch of alienated, dis-oriented, and lost people who desperately needed a Savior. This led to Paul's transition from provocation to proclamation. His anger and arousal didn't turn him into a legalistic, angry "Bible-thumper"—warning everybody to either "turn or burn"—but rather moved him to a place of compassion and reason, because he recognized (with vision) the ability of God to work in hard hearts that are unaware of the gospel.

The apostle Paul went from "worked-up" as he saw the city full of idols, to witnessing the God of all glory and His Son Jesus the Christ. He went from vilifying urban dwellers to being an urban visionary. The question remaining at hand for us as mis-sionaries is this: God is not being worshiped, but what are *we* doing about it?

What we gather from these examples is that each and every member of the body of Christ is commanded to engage in mis-sional living. Moreover, it is an inherent requirement of his or her status as a member of the body of Christ! The very same motiva-tion for Paul's missional engagement exists in each and every be-liever today. As Paul was moved to evangelize, and called others to evangelize, so are we meant to be moved and respond to his call.

Reaching the lost with the gospel is not simply a "cool idea for church growth," but rather a biblical mandate for each of its members. This is the call of the church in every generation—to *equip* all its members for this mission.

MISSIONAL FOCUS

We must have a gospel-centered, intentional, missional focus in the midst of riotousness and rejection. Godlessness is pervasive throughout all our cities—suburban or urban—Jesus Christ must be the centerpiece of this focus, and we must plant His gospel throughout the cities of the world. We see Paul going to the synagogue, the agora, and the Areopagus. The synagogue was Paul's mission to the Jews, the agora was his mission in the marketplace, and the Areopagus was his mission to his present-day culture—where the philosophers and the academics would gather.

First, Paul approached the Jews as part of his strategy. Paul strategically addresses the synagogues with the "God-fearers." Paul sensibly begins there, offering Jesus Christ and His gospel to his *own* people. After that, he went to the Gentiles, who had some acquaintance with the law, worshiped the God of Israel, and inquired further about the gospel; the "God-fearers" did not reject things that they knew came from Moses and the prophets, and so they were drawn closer to the true God (they were explorers)!

After approaching the synagogue, we see another strategy for missional engagement: the agora, or marketplace. Paul went "downtown" to the coffee shops, hookah lounges, restaurants, bookstores, and there he challenged and argued with the regular "hanger-outers" or whoever happened to be there. He went after them every day. By studying his approach, we learn that Paul had consistency and continuity—bringing a continual gospel-presence into the center parts of the city amongst people who don't know Jesus. Throughout Paul's journeys, there was no room for the philosophy, "Us four, no more; bar the door."

What Paul was doing in Athens was demonstrating the necessity of the church to be people-driven and not program-driven. We can learn from Paul, particularly as he was in the agora. Many theologians consider his preaching presence in the marketplace as a "street preacher." Here, in Acts 17, Paul was present in the central *plaza* of the city, proclaiming the message of the cross—telling people in the marketplace the good news of Jesus. Regardless of the type of presence and preaching he demonstrated, the point is that Paul was present, and his presence was one of proclamation in word *and* deed. He preached the gospel, but he was also consistent and continuous in his presence (which leads to deed).

We cannot shrink back from any arena of lostness in our city. In fact, Paul engaged the cultural intellectuals in the Areopagus, which was tantamount to the court or the city council. Paul went "open-air" in the Areopagus without a megaphone, and many people heard of the King and Lord Jesus. As part of his overall strategy for the city, Paul stepped into position to be used by God. On the block we cannot be too afraid, nor too busy, to be strategically positioned to engage lost people; that, in essence, is the purpose of being a missionary *and* on the block! We cannot be so fearful of rejection that we avoid preaching the gospel because people consider us in the same manner they considered the apostle Paul—a "blabbermouth," which means an authoritative-talking fool.

As we feel the weight of the lostness of our city, we must, like Paul, be willing to be rejected, slandered, and misunderstood, all the while pressing forward. In Matthew 16, Jesus teaches that the church stands against the gates of hell (and the gates of hell will not overcome it); it is always charging and advancing—God is on the move. He is sending His church as sheep among wolves. The gospel calls us to death, suffering, rejection, hatred, and humiliation as it charges the gates of hell, so that people who are lost would be found in Christ.

We must take up our cross and get "in step" with Christ, as we invade the culture and its context, and inject the nutrients of the message of the gospel. We must embrace suffering on mission when it comes to reaching our neighborhoods and cities. Jesus is our perfect model in suffering for the sake of others who hated Him. Suffering was a reality for Jesus, and so it is for His followers.

Triumphant suffering (2 Corinthians 8:9) was how Paul described Christ's willingness to charitably give everything to become our everything in his second letter to the church that met in Corinth. We see our Jesus in *sacrificial* suffering (1 Peter 3:18), as He would descend and suffer brutal, tragic murder so that the lost might be reconciled to God.

Also, we see Jesus experience *sanctifying* suffering (Isaiah 53) as He would bear the full weight of what sinful man deserved. He would experience the wounds and the beatings and be crushed by God the Father Himself so that, through His sacrifice, we could receive Him as Lord and King. Although this doesn't call us to *look* for suffering, we must embrace suffering when we experience it, as our Lord has paved the way of suffering in every dimension to lead us into relationship with the Father through His own suffering.

Wesley L. Duewel says powerfully in his book *Ablaze For God*, "Nothing pleases Christ more than for us to share with Him His burden for the world and its people. Nothing so weds us to the heart of Christ as our tears shed as we intercede for lost ones with Him."[3] The stakes are high; we will suffer as we recognize that, apart from the sovereignty of God, no missional engagement will be fruitful.

Paul was asked to give an account of his teaching, and he used the provocation as an opportunity to proclaim; when Paul stood to preach, he used the idols of that city as a platform to reach the people in that city. In other words, Paul *contended* for the faith, and *contextualized* in doing so. Contextualization is an absolute necessity. I'm a firm believer in truly understanding the culture of your area. To serve as effective missionaries in our cities, ministers in particular need a variety of Christian tools— from commentaries, to lexicons, to applied Christianity books on devotion, prayer, and fasting. However, in owning the lostness of our city, we must reside, remain in tune, and be very aware of the culture to which we're preaching Christ.

Yes, I've read and own a copy of *Biblical Theology* by Geerhardus Vos, but I *still* watch B.E.T., peruse the music scene of the most popular hip-hop and R&B artists, and check out a variety of entertainment award shows. Paul also contended and contextualized, as he quoted from a poem in the book of Epimenides and Aratus, similar to the Christopher Hitchens and Deepak Chopra of their day. Nevertheless, in quoting and contextualizing, the apostle Paul never compromised the potency and purity of the message of the gospel.

Here are five ways that Paul addressed his culture:

1. He unveiled the superstition, the idols, of his culture
2. He unveiled the true character of God
3. He exposed how the culture was absent of truth, or "real" reality
4. He revealed that idols cannot represent God
5. He preached Jesus Christ's resurrection

We must take full notice that Paul doesn't lead by attacking their religion unnecessarily, but he exposed to them the erroneous way they thought about God. He didn't pound his culture with doctrine, but rather was patient with others in a sincere posture of grace.

As we missionally engage our blocks, we're not called to "water down" and assimilate into the culture, ignoring the mission of Christ. Paul never changed his position by adapting too much to the culture's philosophies; rather, he preached Christ, and called a superstitious and idolatrous people into the reign of Christ. *Paul didn't change his position; he just changed his pitch.* He threw the gospel at them in a way that they could hear and take in. He hoped they would then consider a more accurate view of the world through the lens of the gospel as Paul struck out their idols; this led to conversion. How was Paul so successful?

Paul unveiled the idols of his culture.

As we missionally engage people with the gospel, we must spend the time assessing the city and the people of the city, with respect to its idols, in order to properly address the issues of the city with sensitivity and realism. It takes a bit of tact, not mere theological brute force.

In multiple contexts, the missionary must both use the elements of culture as a *means* to preach, while contending and contextualizing at the same time:

> Paul's approach to the Colossian syncretism reveals an artistry's sensitivity, not a commander's heavy hand. He refuses to impose a pre-packaged, one-size-fits-all theology and praxis as a guard against syncretism, as sometimes happens today.[4]

We must communicate the gospel in understandable terms appropriate to the audience. This must be the mode of communication for every missionary on the block. There is no such thing as a "one-size-fits-all" presentation of the gospel.

Paul unveiled the true character of God.

He acknowledged their idolatry, and then applied the gospel. The people to whom Paul was speaking were identified as very religious, elaborate idolaters. Using their "unknown" god, he inserted the triune God in their ignorance, and in doing so, he acknowledged the certainty of their uncertainty. That is, when he used the idols of his culture to get into his culture, this "unknown" god got him into their uncertainty about life. *We must point people to a reality beyond what they can see!*

In other words, the apostle Paul was telling the Athenians that their polytheism revealed their uncertainties and insecurities about life (thus, their superstition), and the fact that they've named something the "unknown" god shows that they are *really* uncertain about life's most important questions. Simply, Paul assessed that the Athenians knew for sure they didn't know what they were doing; while pursuing and idolizing knowledge, they were blinded by their own thinking.

> **We've got to get people past the blindness of their ideas, that they might see Christ.**

We've got to get people past the blindness of their ideas, that they might see Christ.

Paul basically says, "I don't want to know anything about y'all but Christ crucified." The gospel is God's plan A. When we enter the block for missional engagement, we have in the front of our minds that God is sovereign and in control, while maintaining a deep care and concern for the lost. We live in the tension between a passion for people and a sincere patience with God's plan. This is a good tension. We cling to the electing power of God to save whomever He wills, while we plow with all of God's energy and love, as our hearts are broken for the lost, and our desire is to see them converted. This tension builds intimacy with God, since we are always making intercession for the lost people in our cities. This tension also keeps us realizing that we cannot look down on lost people, but our love *for* God and the love *of* God work hand-in-hand toward a passionate desire to see Christ in the hearts of the people on the block.

He showed them how uncertain they were.

He presents the *actuality* of God, he poses his *argument* for God, and calls them to *abandon* their mess, and *align* with the God of his argument (1 Thess. 1:9). Paul's goal in his speeches in Paphos, Antioch, and Athens was to introduce his listeners to Jesus, but he used varying tactics based on the cultural context. In the same way, we must be missionally bilingual. He made his argument clear. He called them to abandon their idolatry and align with Christ. Regardless of the content of his argument, he was consistent in his contending, and contextualizing without compromise.

Three camps formed around Paul's teaching. There were those who would mock and heckle him. The second group consisted of those who were motivated to hear more. The third group was made up of a people moved to believe in Jesus. When we step into the weighty lostness of our city, we must remember we will experience different responses, and in my experience these three camps exist all the time. Nevertheless, we're called to be faithful to the mission, faithful to the message, and to be faithful witnesses of the gospel, and in so doing, we believe that God produces fruit as we see in Paul, as Dionysius, Damaris, and others who came to believe the gospel.

In other chapters, I refer to a host of elders at my church, who, with me, breed dogs called American Bullies—prominent in many urban areas of the country, particularly in the inner cities. As we engaged our block, we noticed that many of us had these dogs. We figured then that we might enter into the circles of African American and Latino males who have had multiple American Bullies bred, sold, and displayed at dog shows.

There was a young man named Dequan who I knew for years, and he worked at the shop where I had my car fixed over twenty years. I shared the gospel with him many times over the course of seven of those years. When Dequan would tell me about his many problems, as a war veteran with vehicle accidents that resulted in permanent disability, I shared about Jesus with him on numerous occasions. As I continued to hear the weightiness of his condition, but yet his refusal to receive Jesus as Savior, one day, many years later, as we were laughing and discussing dogs, I invited him to my church, and eventually, he and his girlfriend came to know Christ and were baptized. I contended for the faith, contextualized that they could understand—all driven by the weight of the godlessness of people in my sphere of relationships.

Therefore I, like Paul, was provoked by the many idols being adored in the Christless city, and Jesus Christ not being the centerpiece of the city. So as the stakes are high, and the reality is that many people in my city are going to hell, I am propelled and compelled to preach Christ boldly and continually—risking it all for the least, the last, and the lost on my block.

PART 2

SPEAKING OF CAMDEN

"Camden, New Jersey, stands as a warning of what huge pockets of America could turn into."

CHRIS HEDGES, "CITY OF RUINS,"
THE NATION, NOVEMBER 2010

CHAPTER 5

CAMDEN

I DREAM'D in a dream, I saw a city invincible to the attacks of the whole of the rest of the earth." These are the words that the great poet Walt Whitman said as he reflected upon his resident city. He lived during a time where things were quaint and affluent and was convinced that nothing would overcome the great city where he lived; the same city where I currently reside—Camden, New Jersey. But the Camden I live in is not the one that Whitman wrote about in his poem. If I were to write a poem about my city, it would sound nothing at all like Mr. Whitman's. In fact, it would be the direct opposite.

As a church planter in Camden I have no need to distinguish Camden's inner-city from the rest of it because the whole of the city is plagued with insurmountable challenges. Camden has a violent crime rate seven times higher than the national average. It has ranked in the top violent cities in America for decades. The crime index in Camden is 600 times higher than that of the nation's average. This city has a population of 77,000 people crammed into nine square miles of land. One writer said this of Camden, "Camden is where those discarded as human refuse are dumped."[5]

According to City-Data.com, of the approximately 77,000 people in Camden, 44.8 percent are African American, 45.7 percent Hispanic, and 3.6 percent White; the unemployment rate in the city is about 11 percent, the median household income is $22,043, about 43 percent of the population live below poverty, and about 31 percent of the adult residents have not completed high school. Camden is a city in need. It was rated as the most dangerous city in America in 2015 by NeighborhoodScout.com as reported by NBC Philadelphia. Camden is not Whitman's invincible city. In 2011 the Camden Police Department was forced to cut one-third of officers, and arrests dropped to less than half of what they were in 2009. Camden has led the United States in murder rates several times in the five years my family and I have lived here. The *Huffington Post* said, "Camden is the quintessential unsolvable quagmire of urban plight."[6] And this is where God called me and my family to plant a church.

My original plan was to plant in a neighborhood of Philadelphia, but the Lord called me to Camden through the Holy Spirit's prompting of Dr. Eric Mason and Dr. Phil Ryken. Planting in Camden wasn't a logical decision. For one, I had already pastored in two neighborhoods of Philadelphia, so I was more familiar with the city as a whole. Second, there is no sustainability in Camden. "Camden has long suffered the indignities that poverty breeds."[7]

As my wife, Angel, and I drove through the city of Camden, observing the devastation, brokenness, and abject poverty, we were overwhelmed by the thought of planting a church. Gang wars created streets riddled with gun violence, and young men and women were too often found dead in the street as a result. The dilapidated and abandoned buildings of the city bring about a gloom-and-doom aesthetic to the community. The city has a certain vibe that simply makes people uncomfortable and nervous. The devastation, destruction, and decadence seemed, in the words of Walt Whitman, *invincible.*

During some of those times that we would ride through, we often just pulled our car over and began to talk and share the gospel with random people. As we listened to many people's life stories we became more burdened to see Christ's name be the most famous name in the city of Camden. We wept with the people. We prayed with and for them that God would do a crazy work in and through our future church plant.

I find Isaiah 60 to be a great source of hope toward the future of God's people. This chapter expresses and explains the glorious kingdom that the Lord Jesus Christ will establish when He returns to earth to reign; yet the chapter was written when the people of God were in their seemingly lowest state. Isaiah 60 was written to Israel and Jerusalem at her lowest point, under curse and judgment, seemingly without hope. God gives a vision to His people of how His power can bring new life where death reigns, bring peace where violence overflows, and bring hope where despair grips relentlessly. "The sons of those who afflicted you will come bowing to you, and all those who despised you will bow themselves at the soles of your feet; And they will call you the city of the Lord, the Zion of the Holy One of Israel" (Isaiah 60:14 NASB).

In the passage, the city would be a city of God, a truly invincible city! Farther along in verse 18 it says, "Violence will not be heard again in your land, nor devastation or destruction within your borders" (NASB).

When Angel and I arrived in Camden to plant the church,

the news and all media outlets had pinpointed Camden to be at its lowest point in many years. Three mayors had been removed and prosecuted over the years. The police department was in transition and being taken over by the county. The school district was suffering from a lack of resources and a not-so-good success rate. Murder was at an all-time high and violent crimes were much higher in Camden than the national average. One writer from a major news station reported of Camden that, "On average someone was shot every 33 hours."[8]

The questions we face in the midst of the realities of our city are similar to the realities that the people of God faced in light of their grim and gloomy circumstances. The people of God were living in a devastating ruin—a seemingly hopeless predicament. What is the starting point for a place like this? Where does one look for hope in abject systemic decadence and despair?

The prophet Isaiah preached a sermon that looked into the future and declared a coming, glorious day that the Lord will bring about in His timing. He has not forgotten about them as He stated in Isaiah 60:22, "I am the LORD; in its time I will hasten it." Isaiah teaches us that God can still speak words of life and peace in the midst of hopelessness as he calls for the people of God in Isaiah 60:1 to "arise, shine, for your light has come, and the glory of the LORD has risen upon you. For behold, darkness shall cover the earth, and thick darkness the peoples; but the LORD will arise upon you, and his glory will be seen upon you." It is as if God is calling His people from death to life in this verse. In Isaiah 60:19 He declares a transformed city is coming as He states, "The sun shall be no more your light by day, nor for brightness shall the moon give you light; but the LORD will be your everlasting light." This verse is Holy Ghost caffeine to the worn-out, exhausted, ready-to-give-up, feeling abandoned people of God!

So the next question is, "Why go to Camden (or anywhere like it) in the midst of hopelessness, violence, and a high concentration of poverty?" Beyond the obvious demographic need, there is a pervasive absence of the gospel. Camden is inundated with health-and-wealth theology, which treats the church as a profitable business rather than the prophetic people of God. Many of the churches are more man-centered and pastor-centered than Christ-centered. Some churches faithfully administer the gospel in Camden, but there are simply not enough that do.

> **We are called, much like Isaiah, to preach a message of hope in the midst of despair.**

We are called, much like Isaiah, to preach a message of hope in the midst of despair. We aim as a church plant to preach the powerful, life-changing, sin-killing gospel of Jesus Christ to a people at their lowest point, which is not knowing Christ as Savior! As Isaiah is declaring, the renewal of God's people will come through the power of the Lord. The passage looks forward to a glorious day that will be coming when the Lord Himself will show up and throw His messianic weight around in the earth making all things new.

The passage serves as such a great encouragement to me and it has given me vision for the city of Camden; one perhaps even greater than Whitman's simply because this vision is thrust by the power of God's Messiah—Jesus.

Living in the city, I realized that we must be warriors on the block. There is no room for passivity. There is no room for the church to sit on the bench and function as a lazy consumer, unwilling to risk its life to win people to Jesus. I believe we must have an aggressive and *active* methodology of sharing the gospel with the people of a city like Camden. Without a robust gospel-centered mission, tough cities such as Newark, Detroit, Baltimore, and of course Camden will not see change. God called my family and me to dwell in the city and see this city, and any city for that matter, through the lens of the cross of Christ.

Camden, like many other cities in the United States and the world, is in desperate need of a movement of people who are not just in the four walls of the church, but *on the block*. So through the Father's eternal plan, the Son's magnificent cross-work, and the Holy Spirit's power, my aim in this book is to help you with some practical, biblical, and relevant strategies to invade the darkness of *your* city, neighborhood, and community with a full orbed gospel mission.

We believe that the Word of God compels us to move forward in reaching the world for Christ. Regardless of the influence of violence, poverty, the growth of liberal theology, and the advancement of a man-centered social agenda, we must still be about reaching the least, last, and lost on the block. We long to see the reality of the reign of Christ be realized in Camden. Here we are, Lord! Send us!

I began to dream about what the city would look like with Jesus as the ruler and redeemer reigning over the city. The city in Isaiah 60:18, "Violence shall no more be heard in your land, devastation or destruction within your borders; you shall call your walls Salvation, and your gates Praise."

I have been shown a lot of grace in my life, but I've experienced the highest amount of the grace (as if it is measurable) during my life in this city. There's something special about it. I feel as if the Lord has planned a grand awakening for my city. I can see His hand at work in the city each day, and that only furthers my hope for the future majestic revitalization of other cities around the world. Again, Isaiah 60 presents a city similar to Camden, one of strife, evilness, and neglect. However, the Savior restores all things, no matter what the state. I know that Camden will one day be a restored city—one that won't be such a far cry from the Camden that Whitman knew.

We actively pursue faithful proclamation of the gospel and in tangible works of mercy that will bless all the citizens of our city. But our hope is not ultimately in the revitalization of it. We hope and work for better schools, better streets, better police relations, better jobs, etc. But even if this never happens, we are confident that God has His people here, and that not one of them will perish. The citizens of the city of Camden might never again enjoy the invincible city of Whitman's poem, but we are confident that its citizens will be heirs of the truly "Invincible City" whose builder and maker is God.

STEVIE

When I met Stevie, he was with a girl and they had several kids between the two of them. They had been living together for a long time. Stevie also had the tendency of being high. Over time we became friends, and I would tell him, "man, you need to stop playing. You're in that old city. You need to come over to the new city." The name of our kennel is Nu City Bullies, so that was my joke with people, "Man, get out of that old city and come over to the new city." And he would laugh. I would tell Stevie my prayer for him was that he would submit to Christ and receive Him as Savior and walk away from all the weed. That he would get married to this woman and be a super father, join Nu City Bullies, and join the church. Stevie would always laugh and hug me and say, "Pastor, you're crazy. But you know what, you're the only one who's got any positive thoughts for me, so I really appreciate it. Pastor, I know when you're praying for me because I can feel it when you're praying. Anytime something positive happens, I always say it was Pastor Doug who was praying." And I would say, "I'm not sure about that, but I'm praying you just receive Jesus."

I hadn't spoken to Stevie for a while and I heard he had gotten in trouble with the police. I called him, and when I asked him how he was doing he replied, "Not good. I'm about to do time for these charges." I told him I was on my way to his house so I could pray with him. Given that he also had dogs, I asked him what he wanted to do with them, and he asked if I could help sell them. Over the next week, I nursed his dogs back to health, cleaned them, had a photoshoot with them, and sold one for the price Stevie thought he might get for both. When I gave Stevie his money from the sale, he hugged me, and asked me what was that prayer I always had for him, so I told him: that he would receive Jesus, marry this woman, walk away from drugs, come and join Epiphany Camden, join the new city and get out of this old city. And Stevie said, "I'm feeling like I need to do that."

On the morning that Stevie needed to go to court, he called me, pretty much in tears. Stevie hadn't really been in trouble before. I was already up, so I prayed for him: "I pray, God, that Stevie doesn't wait to see if You're good if he gets less time; that he would see You're good right now, and that in his misery You're still good. I pray that if there's any corruption of his arrest that

You would sniff that out and bring that to light. And God I pray if he's guilty that You would give him the grace to do his time knowing he got what he deserved. But Your mercy is when You don't give him what he deserves and Your grace is when You give him the good that he doesn't deserve." Stevie was just crying on the phone and I told him, "Stevie, go in there in the name of the Lord, trusting that God's decision is more powerful than that judge's."

Stevie called me about six hours later and told me that the cop had acted illegally and they had to throw the case out. Stevie told me he was done with that life.

He called me three days later and said, "Pastor, I received the Lord this Sunday. I went to church and I heard the gospel, man, and it was all that stuff you were saying, and I accepted Christ as Savior. They were going to baptize me, but I told my grandma that I was going to join Epiphany Camden. And I want to join Nu City Bullies and that other life is behind me. Can you help me find a job?" I said, "Absolutely." Glory to God in the highest.

CHAPTER 6

THEM PEOPLE

Growing up in Paterson, New Jersey, I often saw people walking house-to-house, dressed in suit and tie, even in one-hundred-degree weather, carrying little books and briefcases talking about a god they called "Jehovah." As a five-year-old kid I learned that they were called Jehovah's Witnesses. A sad reality in the inner city was that when they would come to the house we would lock the door, hide, and pretend we weren't home instead of engaging them with truth and love. They would leave pamphlets about Jehovah's coming and how to live like Jehovah. How there are 144,000 that are going to go to heaven, as well as information about their publication *The Watchtower*. You could be one of the 144,000 if you placed your allegiance to their hall, which was their picture of Jehovah's world, what they called Kingdom Hall.

For years, they would consistently, intentionally, and aggressively knock, seeking to communicate Jehovah's return and the need to commit our lives to living for Jehovah. I realize that my five-year-old understanding of the Jehovah's Witnesses is somewhat inaccurate, but nonetheless my take-home question was what puzzled me the most: why didn't we go tell people that they should live for Jesus at my African American Baptist Church? We prayed to Jesus, we worshiped Him, and we sang songs about Him, yet none of my Christian friends, their parents, deacons, preachers, nor even the Logan household would go aggressively and intentionally tell people to get ready for Jesus' return.

Remembering this contrast in my own church growing up, and even as I became a pastor myself, I realized that I saw my Christianity primarily flowing out of "insider life." Everything was done inside the walls of the church building. The people who weren't Christians were considered "them people," but we were "God's people." So I was always taught not to be like those wicked people out there, but to be like these holy people in here. What kept coming back to my mind as a young, churchgoing kid was, "How come we don't tell *them* wicked people about Jesus so that they might become holy people, like the Jehovah's Witnesses do?"

Poor strategy affected my ministry as I began my career as a thirty-two-year-old minister at a small Plymouth Brethren Church in the Kensington section of Philadelphia. I was utterly dumbfounded as to how I was going to grow this church. I began to invite my friends to come and join us. When two or three did, it still left me with only twenty-three people. I was forced to figure out how in the world I was going to grow a church for the glory of God. I soon realized that I had not been taught how to missionally engage a community with the gospel for the purpose of seeing the lost become found in Christ, and helping them to grow from spiritual infancy to spiritual maturity.

I was clueless, and I realized I had an unclear definition of missional engagement and discipleship. I had clearly not experienced either of these things through training at my former church.

As I began to look back, I wondered if there had ever been an emphasis to reach the lost in our preaching, in our singing, and in our ministry. All this affected my preaching, my teaching, my disciple-making, and particularly my view and practice of evangelism.

> **The church, when it seeks to engage and agonize over its community, must *know* the community intimately.**

By God's grace, the clarification of what was missing came to me one day while I was listening to the song "Ain't Nobody Worryin'" by Anthony Hamilton. Anthony is a soul and R&B singer from Charlotte. He sings earnestly and beautifully about the problems facing his community. He sings of gunshots, sirens, death, suffering, homelessness, hunger, poverty, poor education, crime, unemployment, and yet "ain't nobody worryin'."

When Anthony Hamilton sings of the pain of his neighborhood, he does not use his imagination. The children dying, the mothers crying, the rampant strife on the street—these are not conjured up images that came to him in a dream. Rather, they are real concerns of real people. He sings about the pain of his block because he *knows* the pain on his block. In just the same manner, the church, when it seeks to engage and agonize over its community, must *know* the community intimately.

Suddenly the missing component of my ministry dawned on me. My ministry lacked the appropriate sense of *agony*. Agony for the community into which I had entered. Agony for my neighbors who were suffering and broken. Agony over my willingness to be comfortably distant.

For all my theoretical learning, the great Christian truths I had learned, my ministry lacked heart. I was on an abstract mission, not one that actually reached into communities with the appropriate love and care it requires. Though I sought to reach the least, the last, and the lost through the gospel, I was emotionally disconnected. I did not experience the community's pain, nor did I personally invest myself in its healing and salvation.

Mission does not simply amount to a profession of theological truths in new contexts. We cannot hope for the mere intellectual salvation of community members, abstractly hoping that they will hear our speeches and come to Christ. Instead, we must enter into communities physically and emotionally. We must enter into their suffering and speak the gospel into their individual, broken contexts. We cannot effectively serve broken people and bring them the gospel unless we know their brokenness.

This realization motivated me to expand my understanding of the gospel ministry in the urban context. The practice of urban missions is extremely difficult. Urban communities face the relentless terrors of senseless violence, broken families, poor education, and inadequate housing. How does one enter into a fully orbed mission in such a context? I believe the answer begins with a commitment to engage in a ministry that is marked by agony— that feels the pain, confusion, and darkness of the community it desires to see saved. It is a love for our communities that follows the example of the empathetic love of Jesus.

Urban ministry will not succeed if we continue to make the false dichotomy between *them people out there* and *us people in here*. It must be all of us together, feeling each other's pain, carrying each other's burdens, agonizing in the trenches of real life battles and suffering, caring deeply for one another.

In a city such as Camden, flooded with idols—immersed,

swamped, saturated with every god but Jesus—how do you plan on living out the gospel in the community? It is a community that is hostile to the true and living God, and thus, hostile to one another as well. How are you going to pump out the toxic and acidic idols of Satan's age-old schemes to cripple and corrupt the people of *your* city?

SCOTTIE

Scottie had spent time in jail for felonies. When he got out, he was invited regularly to Epiphany Philly, where I previously served as a pastor and out of which I planted. He was not into it at all, but because he was trying to do better and, as he would say, trying to be positive, he did visit. Scottie's brother and sister came with me as part of my original launch team coming out of Epiphany Philly and planting in Camden. His brother and sister continued inviting him, so Scottie finally came over one day to my yard and saw that the growing congregation was just loaded with people from Camden. It was interesting for him so he would hang around. I shared the gospel with him, asking him about receiving Christ but he kept saying, "Nah, I'm good. I love what y'all are doing but that's for y'all, not for me."

However, he came to the official launch worship service. The next morning, Scottie knocked on my door and asked if he could talk with me. As exhausted as I was, I invited him in and asked him, 'What's on your heart, brother?" He said, "Man, I received the Lord yesterday. The message pierced my heart. I want to walk with Jesus, and I want to walk with y'all. Tell me what I need to do. I'm looking for a wife and I'm saving my money. I'm about to get a house and get my life together." I rejoiced with him. And when he told me he played the guitar, I told him, "Walk with Pastor T." We do what we call synchronized discipleship; if you're a worship team–type I'm going to put you with my worship pastor. So Pastor T and I walked with Scottie for several months. He grew in leaps and bounds and played the guitar for the church. A short time later, he came to me desiring to marry a young lady in our church. She was like a daughter to me, and I gave him the green light to have the conversation with her. She said yes, and they were married. In addition, he was ordained as a deacon because he was serving viably and actively. So within six years of his receiving Christ, Scottie was baptized, got married, and ordained as a deacon. He continues to walk in discipleship and also disciples others on the worship team. He and his wife are also a mentoring couple for newly married couples.

Prior to his coming to the Lord, Scottie saw God as *a* power but not *the* power; he seemed to see God but did not see God high and lifted up. Scottie always had a decent respect and view of God, but what I didn't get from him initially was that he didn't see God as ultimate; he saw God as great and good, but not ultimate. My prayer for Scottie from the get-go was that he would see there is no God in positive living, and that he would only see Christ high and lifted up and mighty to save. I wanted Scottie to see his deep need for a Savior. I wanted him to realize that his sins had separated him from God and he needed Christ to save him, not just some so-called "positivity." Once he came to that launch worship service where there was celebration and exaltation and preaching—Scottie eventually conveyed to me, "Man, I never saw God like that. Pastor Doug, it was crazy. The Lord just kept messing in my heart and, man, He just saved me. And I was rejoicing."

CHAPTER 7

BEGINNING ON
THE BLOCK

One of my favorite hip-hop groups in the mid-nineties was De La Soul. They came out with an album called *Stakes Is High*. This album was, in many ways, very different from their previous releases. *Stakes Is High* dealt with many topics and themes, particularly the state of the hip-hop world in their era by analyzing and criticizing the current condition of the hip-hop world. They saw that hip-hop culture and music had become overwhelmingly commercialized, attributing the commercialization to the rise and infiltration of "gangsta rap." Following the album, many dissenting opinions to De La Soul's assessment and critique of the state of hip-hop culture and music arose.

When I see the state of the church's lack of passion for missional engagement, it is much like the way De La Soul saw the origins of hip-hop being annihilated from next generation hip-hop "gangsta rap." Just as the origins of hip-hop were being lost to an emerging style of rap culture, so must Christ's church see the annihilation of passion for missional engagement (a passion for the "lostness" of our cities today) in today's Christian subculture—certainly antithetical to the intended *modus operandi* of the church that God intended in His Word.

When I am out on my block in Camden, I see that the stakes are high for the church regarding people who are separated from Christ. The stakes are high when I view the pain of the many single-parent homes in which children long for a mother *and* a father—replaced by grandmothers who act as their new single parents. The stakes are high as I see many young men caught up in gang violence, craving a role model or father figure, and giving into gang members who are happy to oblige them with corrupt living in the name of "family," and "keeping it 100." The stakes are high when I see the young lady who was only planning on "selling" her body "a few times" to get back on her feet and to provide for her children, but sadly gets caught up in years of prostitution. The stakes are high when I see myriad children struggling with hunger and homelessness every day in my city. I, too, have been guilty of not being about reaching the block and seeing the comprehensive transformation of people in my city through the gospel.

I remember visiting another church as we were getting ready to launch Epiphany Fellowship in Camden back in 2011. At that stage of our church plant, we met for worship at five in the evening. Often, I would visit partner churches for worship on Sunday mornings. A pastor one morning preached a message, a very doctrine-soaked message. He began to talk about the troubles and trials in his city, in the suburban context very close to the city of Camden. The pastor proceeded to speak of issues in Camden as well, and how the pervasive godlessness in Camden upset him.

After the sermon, an elder came to me, and asked me where I was from, to which I responded, "Paterson, New Jersey, but I'm planting a church in Camden." He questioned, "Who with?" An interesting question, but I played along, and responded, "Tenth Presbyterian Church and Epiphany Fellowship Church out of Philadelphia."

"Oh, you're Presbyterian?"

"Yes."

"Well you know, people in Camden won't receive Presbyterians; we've tried for years, but they won't accept our standards [the Presbyterian *Book of Church Order* and the Westminster Confession of Faith]. Many African Americans are Baptist and Pentecostal in Camden, and they don't want anything to do with Reformed theology. We've tried for years, and we sort of just gave up going out to witness to them."

So, I charitably conveyed to the pastor that I preach a *gospel*-centered (not a Presbyterian-centered) message; I try to raise *gospel*-centered (not Presbyterian-centered) disciples. Reformed theology is simply *biblical* theology expressed and explained, and we've seen people come to Christ even at our early gatherings through missional engagement in some of the roughest streets in Camden.

But this pastor had given up. He did not recognize that the stakes were high for the lost people in Camden. He tried; it didn't seem to work, so he quit. The godlessness of the city of Camden did not provoke this brother sufficiently to proclamation, but rather pushed him to give up on our city. He lacked that clarity of vision fueled by the Great Commission of Christ that the apostle Paul demonstrated in the godless streets of Athens. And in a sense, the block quelled his vision, whereas the disciples that Jesus calls are to maintain a call and vision that missionally shape the city.

In Acts 17, Paul was driven toward missional engagement by the godlessness of the city. The provocation that Paul experienced through the Christlessness of Athens sparked him beyond just wishful thinking and passive despair. He conversed with Epicurean and Stoic philosophers, many of whom considered him a nut-job for preaching about a resurrected Jesus. Paul had in mind, during his encounter in Athens, the person of Jesus Christ as the centerpiece to replace the gods with (literal) clay feet in the city. He had in mind the power of Jesus to transform hard hearts and convert unbelievers. He didn't immediately jump to strategizing so much as he proceeded to proclaiming the true God and Savior. In the same way, we must have Jesus—His character, power, humility, boldness, and all that He has done to redeem fallen man—as the centerpiece of our evangelism. Robert Plummer states,

> This picture of the crucified Christ serves as a constant reminder that a horrific death was needed to rectify humanity's desperate state. The crucifixion declares both the awesome love of God and the miserable "failing grade" that even the best of fallen human behavior deserves (i.e., the punishment Christ received was the just penalty for even the finest of human religiosity).[9]

I believe that the pastor of the church I visited that one Sunday had great intentions. He seemed to be a very godly man. He did attempt to go into the dangerous streets of Camden with the gospel, and maybe God called him away; not all of us are called to go there. Sometimes, consistent rejection of the gospel in any city can be hard for us as missionaries in our cities. But as Plummer states in his book, the picture of the crucified Christ is our *constant reminder* of the weight of humanity's desperate situation, arousing constant provocation in our souls—leading to proclamation. *That's* what led to Paul's proclamation. Jesus Christ demonstrated for us a character of steadfastness as He faced the world's ultimate rejection, the cross! He modeled this as He faced the ultimate rejection of the Father on the cross as He was made a sacrifice for the remission of sins. He remained faithful to reach those rejecting Him, and painted us a beautiful, scandalous picture for the *ultimate* Missionary: one who came passionately aroused by the godlessness of the block, only to become the substitutionary casualty of those to whom He was ministering, while proclaiming the coming of the kingdom of God to *restore* the block.

The pastor was somewhat grieved by the sins in Camden and aroused to speak about the sins and godlessness of Camden in his sermons, yet he was not aroused to action. He was mesmerized by the mess, but not moved by the Messiah. The gospel prevents us from just being angry and aroused; the gospel motivates us by God's Holy Spirit to be *engaged* on the block. Therefore, the proper response to the gospel would be a *motivation* to see God's name made the most famous in our cities (and in all the earth)! We've got to do more than *identify* the pervasive idols in our communities. We must be intentional about our plans for the *implementation* of missional engagement in our urban communities.

We must view missions along the great, redemptive trajectory that was set forth from the beginning. Dr. Steve Childers says, "*God has ordained that His kingdom comes with transformational power into every sphere of life, primarily through the Church,*"[10] and that ordination was proclaimed from the beginning. This is the heart of God. Therefore, this must be the heart of every Christ follower.

Armed as I was by much rich teaching, I must admit that I was missing something when the time came to actually practice what I had been taught. As I attempted to preach the gospel to the least, last, and the lost, I had a sense that I was not equipped with a full tool kit. It was a time of confusion and self-doubt. I had received expert training, and yet felt as though part of me was still not ready.

When we got to Camden, the neighborhood hangout happened to be the basketball court behind our house. However, it was an eyesore. People used to dump garbage and furniture in the field right next to the court. We decided that this beat-up, messed-up, and drug-infested center of family life needed rehabilitation. I went to the city and asked to rebuild it, but they didn't have funds for it. I called church partners to raise money and recruit volunteers to rebuild the court, both for its immediate impact as well as an investment in Camden's future. After calling a few partner churches, people began to show up and the money started coming through.

Everybody on the block was talking about the courts being redone; they thought I personally owned the basketball court! One morning, we ran out of supplies. I prayed for favor from the store, then we drove there with three trucks and filled several carts full of materials. I told the cashier to call his manager, whom I had befriended. I told him: "I don't have money and I have $5,000 worth of stuff and I can't pay." (I had only $800.) My friend approved the donation. I'll never forget the cashier handing me the phone again and the manager saying, "Pastor Doug, you owe me. . . but all you owe me is prayer." God honored our risky step of faith. The Department of Public Works even saw us working and got approval for ten city workers to get paid overtime while helping us for three days. All in all, it took ninety hours of volunteer work from fifty volunteers, as well as eight garbage trucks and three full Dumpsters.

After the grand opening of the court, we had an opening game with the video cameras running. One young man started threatening the other players. When one of the guys barely fouled him, he went to grab his gun and we had to call the police. Two days later, a bunch of kids tried to bend the basketball rims down and spray paint the backboards. After we built up the courts, the devastation in unchanged hearts threatened to tear it down again. Through this

Reconstruction is an unending, lifelong process.

experience God reminded us that reconstruction is an unending, lifelong process. We are always building and rebuilding on the block. As Hebrews 11:8–10 tells us, "By faith Abraham, when called to go to a place he would later receive as his inheritance, obeyed and went, even though he did not know where he was going. By faith he made his home in the promised land like a stranger in a foreign country; he lived in tents, as did Isaac and Jacob, who were heirs with him of the same promise. For he was looking forward to the city with foundations, whose architect and builder is God" (NIV).

We are to build and rebuild the urban areas until we die, or Jesus returns and chauffeurs us to the city of God in heaven. I can hardly wait for that, but while we await one of these two outcomes we must do the work of comprehensive building in our cities.

Rebuilding a city has to start with acknowledging its brokenness. Before planting Epiphany Camden in 2012, my wife and I used to take weekly prayer walks or prayer drives through the city. As I mentioned before, we would talk to folks walking down the sidewalk and hear their stories. My wife and I hurt for them.

One woman, with tears in her eyes, told us about a traumatic event that had happened to her twenty years earlier as if it had occurred yesterday. She had never been able to move forward.

We met a high school student who had been on the "who's who" list of New Jersey graduating seniors, and one of the top five students of her class at Camden High. With this accomplishment—she was working in fast food. We made arrangements to connect her to a college which in turn offered her a full scholarship. But she rejected the offer because she felt that staying at the fast food restaurant in the hood was a better plan for her life. She simply couldn't see herself outside of the devastation because it was all she knew.

We talked to another high school student. His grandmother was in ministry and told him because he continued to sin that he was a reprobate and God could not save him. We tried to tell him that "what is impossible with man is possible with God" (Luke 18:27). Instead of accepting the truth he accused us of attacking his grandmother. His grandmother was the only person who had shown him love, so he chose to stick with her perversion of the truth over trusting the Word of God. One after another these encounters broke me. Nehemiah and Jesus wept for Jerusalem. I wept for Camden. I wept as I experienced firsthand, live and direct, the systemic effects of abject poverty, the impact of a long-term subpar education system, and the darkness of the false gospel that had its grip on the dwellers of my city. I wished I had a magic wand so I could transform this suffering place.

I began to realize this would be the hardest work I would ever do. I wanted to pick up and find a new, less broken city in which to plant a church. But like Nehemiah, I gained a new perspective on the city. My wife and I came to the realization that these problems could never fix themselves. God was calling us to be local and present in the heart of suffering Camden for the long haul as Christ's ambassadors.

YOUNG JUDAH

Judah was what I'd call the person of peace. He was one of the first people I met on the block when I moved to my neighborhood. He started hanging over at my house during my home rebuilding process and eventually just started helping me. He led a group of people on the block who bred American Bullies. I bred dogs, too, so he introduced me to his breed and we began talking about that. Over time, we began talking about Jesus. Judah wanted to know how I'm a pastor, but I'm wearing Polo shirts and Timberlands. In that process, I began sharing the gospel with him constantly.

I shared with him about the church. He was there when we had our first church core group meeting. He was there at almost every Bible study and meeting we had. And we continued to ask Judah about whether he wanted to receive Jesus. His reply was honest, clear, and often littered with foul language! The gist for our purposes here was "Nah, forget that. I don't really mess with the church or with Jesus like that. I just really love y'all!" And that went on for a year.

Judah was a well-known felon throughout Camden. Over time, he trusted me enough to let me help him turn himself in for an assault charge. He spent almost a year in prison. During the time he was incarcerated I sent him my manuscript for my sermon every week. Every now and again, I would pray with him on the phone when he called and I would ask him if he wanted to receive Christ, but he would say, "Nah, I'm good." I was praying that Jesus would draw Judah to Him. And then one week, I forgot to send him my sermon manuscript and he called me (collect, of course), and he said, "Yo, why you ain't sending me my sermon?" I apologized and told him I'd send it to him, but I quipped I had already sent so many and that he hadn't read all of them.

Judah replied, "Man, I teach Bible study at the jail." In jest I responded, "How is your unsaved, heathen-self going to teach a Bible study?" He said, "The Lord saved me a couple weeks ago. I've been teaching Bible study up here with your sermons." He received the Lord in prison and led a couple of people to Christ in prison. When he came home, I baptized him.

The overall sense of his initial rejection of the gospel was that he didn't get it. He'd say, "I heard you say it, you explained it, but I just didn't get it." Then one day in his jail cell reading 1 Peter and sermon manuscripts of the 1 Peter series I was preaching through at that time, Judah simply said that somehow he just got it. An additional point that was hard for Judah to initially reconcile in his mind was my nontraditional approach as a pastor. Even though Judah was turned off by the traditional church and pastors he was familiar with, he was in many ways stranded between my ultracontemporary pastoral style and his growing up in a highly traditional African American Baptist church. Judah conveyed that he thought folks from the highly traditional context he knew were fake; in contrast, he said I was real but that my approach was so "not church." "It's just like love and friendship and family; it didn't feel like church," he would say. Judah was expecting things to turn bad by everything becoming like the highly traditional realm that he remembered, but things never did.

You may be wondering what allowed me to allow a felon into my home. No more, no less. I'm from the "hood." If you're on the block, you start hanging with folks, and you're going to invite them in. God has given me the grace to disarm people with jokes, which allows people to feel close to me very quick. Along with Judah, there are others on the block who, upon learning I was a pastor, were comfortable enough with me to say, "Pray for me, man. I got these charges coming. And I don't really know any pastors so to have one on the block to kick it with, man, that's good." At the time, Judah was helping with my home rebuilding. He was dealing with some charges, and that was the basis of one of our first conversations, which led to one of our first prayers—for the charges he was dealing with. And as we finished my home rebuilding, Judah took pride in having had a hand in it, and had a sense of accomplishing it with us. He then began to introduce me to his people as his friend and his pastor—to Muslims, to drug dealers, to thugs, to crack addicts.

Judah and I would pray together as we sat down to share meals together, when I would say to him, "We're about to eat this food. How can I pray for you?" For me, missional living means always praying Colossians 4, for doors to open for the Word. Regarding Judah, I was praying, "God, put me in the greatest vantage point to show Judah the cross at the greatest vantage point." Sometimes my big personality would get in the way because people see me and love me and they know I'm a Christian who loves Jesus and they would be my friend; and Judah was my friend because we laughed and joked and I'm a clown. But I didn't want that to clown Jesus, so my prayer was often, "God, put me in a position to give You the biggest light, not my jokes." Another thing I was praying throughout was from 2 Corinthians 4, that God would remove the blinders of the evil one and that Judah would see the light of the gospel.

In my city, my hope is for God to work among indigenous unbelievers so that He would raise indigenous church leaders. My prayer is for God to convert and raise up people like Judah who, by God's grace, have been discipled to the point of becoming indigenous leaders *in* the context, *from* the context. With Judah, discipleship was more than just a relationship with me. He was with everybody on my church plant core team as we would go to dog shows together and as we did cookouts. Judah went with me to church planting community meetings. He went with me when I had an out-of-state preaching engagement. This was all even before he became a Christian! Tons of believers were hanging around him the whole time.

As Judah was hanging often at my house, word got back to his father that Judah was hanging with a pastor. His father, a Christian, was in utter disbelief because the son he knew had no pastor, didn't attend church, and hung with ex-cons. To confront his son in what was surely a lie, Judah's father drove the forty-five minutes from where he lived to my house. But upon meeting me and learning where I was from and hearing about the church we had planted, and as we were talking about Jesus, Judah's father started to cry, hugged me, and reached over to his son. He then called Judah's older sister who lives close by to come over and told both his kids to listen and learn from me. He warned them that if he heard that they were giving me a problem that they would have to deal with him. Judah's sister also heard and couldn't believe that he was a Christian and had started coming to the church, as did his brother, and they were both ministered to by the congregation.

Their parents would come visit our church once in a while also. So there was a comprehensive engagement in dealing with Judah all the way through to his whole family.

I could easily have stood back and dismissed Judah as one of *them people*. He was too dangerous. He is not the church type. He would never listen to the gospel, much less respond. Judah was known not only on the block but throughout my city for his prior dealings. But in Judah's story, we see God shining the light of the gospel in even the most hardened of hearts. Yes, people come to Christ all the time but here with Judah we see a remarkable example of God raising someone up *in* the context, *for* the context in a powerful way.

CHAPTER 8

MOVEMENT

"For the church to live out an intimate engagement with the narrative of God's action in Jesus Christ that shapes its life and thought, it must use personal and communal ways of knowing that reach beyond the merely rational."[11]
—Leslie Newbigin

The absence of God's name in the city, in this present reality, is God's sovereign rigging for the church planter that makes generational discipleship our goal and song. As a result, we are drawn to the void to make disciples for God's mission. I like to call them "missional" disciples because the city will never be whole in this life—it will never reach God's intended shalom state in the present world; thus, the disciples we empower are called to engage the city on mission with God's message of shalom, nonetheless, to lead people to the city "with foundations, whose architect and builder is God" (Hebrews 11:10).

On our journey to develop biblical principles for missionally engaging the block, let's look at some practical ways this can be accomplished. I've served in the urban context for more than a decade, and through trial and error, prayer, fasting, cultural exegesis, and the needs of the culture in which I serve, I've put together varying assortments of outreach events. To my point, Christopher Wright says this, "The reality is, of course, as soon as you think seriously about it, that the mission field is everywhere, including your own street—wherever there is ignorance or rejection of the gospel of Jesus Christ."[12] Therefore, these are annual events, monthly events, and day-to-day presence evangelism strategies.

Many of these principles and strategies put you directly in the midst and middle of the messy parts of your city. Many of these strategies will make nonconfrontational, introverted, and even extroverted people very uncomfortable. They are designed to put you on the frontline, high-traffic areas of the city in the places of the highest needs, whatever that may be. The hope is that we won't find comfort in the safety of our familiar settings. Rather, the hope is that God will stretch and grow us in the exploration of uncharted waters in our cities where we are forced to rely on and find peace in Christ. I pray that the fear of rejection, violence, and discomfort will be replaced by the joy of seeing people meet Jesus and the neighborhood improved through the church's service.

These are some of the events and strategic missional engagement principles I've worked with to be a blessing to our congregation, our city, and future generations, but they are by far not the only ones. These are the things I had in mind as I sought to lead my congregation and my city with long-term, ongoing strategy in leadership development—so please see this list as what we did, not as what should necessarily be done in your context.

Morning Manna

We have something called Morning Manna, where we set up at high-traffic bus stops and give away free coffee, donuts, and healthy snacks for the kids on their way to school. We offer prayer, Bibles, and yes we do invite them to our church. We've been able to engage thousands of people monthly through this ministry.

Church-School Partnerships

As part of our Connections Ministry, we are in good relationship with several schools in the neighborhood where our church building is located. We provide school uniforms for kids in need, serve food at the schools for student-conferences, do mentoring, and help with utility bills, food, and clothing.

Local Sports

We like to get involved in the local sports. We connected with the organizer of the Little League Baseball Association and asked how we could come alongside them in an area of need. One of our pastors wound up coaching a team, and we gave financially toward some equipment they needed to have a successful and fun season for the youth of our community.

Community Day

We've also started a Community Day that has been a big joy to our congregation and to the city. We set up a triage in our church building and parking lot, and we've had medical missions for health screenings, diabetes, blood pressure, and asthma. On that day, it's really just a big barbecue with services to contribute to the betterment, short- and long-term, of the people in our neighborhood and community. We give out free haircuts where we incorporate local barbers donating their time and services, along with healthy hygiene packs of soap, toothpaste, etc., to support anyone in our community who is in need. The pastor over Connections has multiple training sessions with the principles of "on the block." We've taught it to our members and we've implemented it by way of our Connections Ministry, and from the pulpit to each and every member of our church. God has been faithful to raise up people who were formerly timid, and fearful of confrontation and connection with strangers, but by God's grace people are stepping out on faith, as they've seen God bring plenty of people to know Jesus through this ministry. The goal of our Connections Ministry was to create a high-volume, high-traffic arena, where we could do random acts of kindness, deeds of mercy that create means of opportunity for us to meet, love, and serve our neighbors with the gospel of Jesus Christ.

Church Plant Residency

It is our goal not just to develop our particular congregation for missional engagement on the block but to expand that to various other cities in the nation. One way in which we seek to accomplish that by God's grace is through the planting of churches. We started a Church Plant Residency program the same year we planted Epiphany Camden, and we have worked and developed planters who have gone to other urban contexts, primarily on the East Coast in places like Philadelphia, Baltimore, Miami, and Wilmington, Delaware. These wonderful men of God I got to serve as my sons in the ministry absorbed with great fervor the teachings of church planting, which encompassed the vision for missional engagement in the streets. Front-loaded into our church plant training are the "on the block" strategies that they are to implement into their regular discipleship in their cities, that we might increase effectiveness of reaching the lost in all regions across the nation, to that end, by God's grace.

Thriving

Thriving is an urban ministry resource collaboration in which Dr. Eric Mason serves as president, and I serve on the board. The hopes and intentions behind Thriving were for the purpose of collaborating with any church planter who desires to participate, but more specifically, the urban minority church planter who lacks resources in engaging their city. So we've sought to collaborate with other networks, denominations, and churches on our mission to strengthen churches that are seeking help in being more effective in reaching their city with the gospel. We have an annual gathering called the Frequency Conference, where church leaders of all races and places come to Philadelphia to be invested in, encouraged, and have access to resources that will aid them in their development as urban leaders. By God's grace, I've taught "on the block" principles there each of our first four years, and it's always a joy to hear from many people across the country how it was a blessing to them.

Acts 29

The Acts 29 Network is a church-planting network that we are pleased to be a part of. I've been in and around the Acts 29 Network for nearly a decade and serve on the leadership team for the North Atlantic Network that spans from Maine to Charlottesville, Virginia. The tagline for Acts 29 is a "diverse, global family of church-planting churches." Acts 29 has been instrumental in funding many inner-city churches. I've spoken at many Acts 29 conferences and I've been often asked to speak particularly on missiology. It has been my joy to serve this great group of godly men who have sought to engage cities across the world with the gospel. Furthermore, it has been my pleasure to communicate the great need for missional engagement in every city and every corner on the globe. I've sought to invest through preaching at these conferences and doing workshops, and that will continue, as Acts 29 journeys on planting gospel-centered churches across the world.

"On the Block" Collective

Along with several pastors and church leaders that I deeply trust, godly men and women of God, I have been encouraged to develop an "On the Block" resources collaborative, where these principles and strategies could be quantified into not just a book, but a plethora of outlets to get them to the maximum amount of people:

- On the Block Blog: This is where I'll be expressing some daily activities of life and mission in my city along with several other pastors who will be blogging from their cities with me across the nation, from both suburban and urban contexts, encouraging church leaders with current, relevant stories about how God met them in sharing the gospel to their specific context. Pastors like Rich Rivera in the Bronx, JR Vassar in Grapevine, TX, Chris Atwell in Charlottesville, VA, and Ernest Grant in Camden, NJ. I hope this crazy array of stories inspires and encourages people to keep at the hard work of engaging the least, the last, and the lost in their cities no matter how difficult it may prove.

- On the Block Music: Though I have no musical talents other than writing a song or two during a sermon series with my worship pastor, I think music is a great median to communicate the truths of Scripture in an instrumental, melodic way. This book will come equipped with an album, where I seek to do that in a real tangible way. I have a collection of godly and talented musicians, singers, and rappers who will be making regular contributions of original songs and hymns that will speak to the urban reality of mission in rugged cities across America. I hope to release new music monthly that will have a robust gospel proclamation, and a robust relevant picture of the landscape of mission in inner cities and other cities.

• On the Block Conference: This will be an annual gathering of speakers and leaders from across the country from all contexts, in which we'll gather to serve pastors and leaders from all over the country. There we will teach multiple segments of the on the block principles and strategies that are outlined in this book. As a young pastor and church planter, I attended many conferences during seasons in my ministry when I was ready to quit, and I heard from many people at these conferences who encouraged me in the Lord to continue in the faith to the mission of the streets. We pray that this conference will be a blessing to many leaders, urban and suburban. We pray that it would give principal points to create a deeper longevity, an increased effectiveness, and help to maximize the leader's potential to be a better pastor and missionary to their context. The conference will have crazy music concerts, books, videos, music packets, and a variety of other ministries that desire to contribute toward the greater effectiveness of ministry leaders across the country. This is my desire—to leave a legacy of grace to my children and grandchildren long after I'm gone. By God's grace, the adoption of on the block principles through this conference will be simply the outworking of the Great Commission and owning the lostness of our cities, all to the glory of God to see many and any trust Christ as Savior.

I pray that these missional strategies and ideas that we have utilized for our city will be useful and tweakable for your community. Again, these strategies have not always gone as well as we thought they would, but God met us in them and blossomed them by His power and not our grand strategy. We take great comfort in the use of these strategies as they are not ultimate but Christ's sovereignty and grace is at work in us in the missional engagement of our block and yours anywhere on the globe.

PATRICK

Patrick came up through Christian hip-hop and hung with all the Christian rappers out of a great church in New York City since he was there when they first launched. For many years he was a Christian rapper, himself. When his father became terminally ill, though, Patrick started to fall apart a bit. He was rapping at a lot of churches but emotionally, relationally, maturity-wise there was little discipleship. So one day, he went with a friend to go buy some weed, but instead his friend got robbed. When they started arguing, Patrick got stabbed in the back. He was rushed to the hospital and almost died. His church had about forty people in the hospital lobby praying and fasting all night for Patrick's healing. He came out of surgery, but Patrick just walked away from the Lord. By the time his father died from his illness not too much later, Patrick was done with God. He became a heavy weed smoker and drinker and philanderer.

When I moved to Camden to plant our church, I happened to move close by to Patrick. He happened to be walking down the street on his way to a weed spot when he saw me and exclaimed in disbelief, "What you doin' here on my block?!?" I told him that I bought a house there. He replied, "I'm doing everything in my power to get away from Jesus and His church, and then He has you move on my block. This ain't good." So he tried to avoid me. But I would just sit on the stoop, since I didn't yet have an office. And I would see him, and he'd finally stop and we'd talk. I'd share the gospel with him. We'd go get breakfast or lunch. Over time, we had an ongoing joke when I would see him heading to the corner store and I would jest, "You better get some ice from the store because hell is hot!" In seriousness, though, I would challenge him like father-to-son. I challenged him to stop smoking weed because it didn't honor the Lord. He contended that he was a Christian—even though he didn't go to church, pray, read the Bible, or have any relationship with Christ—because he accepted Christ when he was three years old. We went through what the Bible had to say about that. And then one Sunday, he just came to church. And after several visits, he really received the Lord and was baptized not long after, and then we started to disciple him.

Some of the guys on the block—the weed dealers and the smokers—tried to convince Patrick to walk away from the Lord because they considered the church fake, but he just kept pushing back. They scoffed at Patrick, saying he would be back smoking sooner or later, and that he wasn't a real Christian and that I was a fake. Sometimes they would take a different tactic, saying he wasn't so bad that he needed Jesus. He's held tough, though he's had his slips, but he's held tough. Patrick has traveled with me to preaching engagements throughout the country, since we as pastors never travel to a city alone. We would go through Greg Gilbert's *What is the Gospel?* and then follow that up with *Christian Beliefs: Twenty Basics Every Christian Should Know*, and through Scripture. Patrick has also written almost an album-full of Christian hip-hop songs.

My prayer early on for Patrick was that God would show him he wasn't a Christian. I didn't even know how to pray that but that's how I prayed—that God would make this clear to Patrick. One of the biggest hindrances in the urban context is "easy believe-ism," that walking the aisle or praying when you were four years old makes you a Christian. And it never wears off in many people's minds. And therefore my prayer for Patrick was, "Lord, make it evident that You're absent from him so that he can have a real need for You. And as Patrick struggles at times to be a good father to his own son, let him know You, God, that You are a good Father and that You care for him enough to make clear to him that Patrick isn't a son but needs to be made a son. Let Patrick know that spiritually he is living a Father-less life."

In the daily flow of missional living is missional engagement.

Besides me, Pastor T, Deacon Patrick, and Charlie Mitchell (one of our church planters in residence) have also been instrumental in walking with Patrick and helping set a solid example of a life with the good Father. He joined their DNA group and went through the book *Unleashed* by Dr. Eric Mason. His discipleship consisted of him becoming a missional disciple himself. And as with all our new members, Patrick was equipped to read Scriptures and handle Scriptures not for the sake of being argumentative with those who disagreed on any given proof text, but to help see and help others see clearly, and win them to the heart of the gospel from Genesis to Revelation.

Though we overlapped some while we were together at the church in NYC, I hadn't really thought to actively pursue Patrick when I was planting in Camden. Having said that, missional living is just doing life in the neighborhood and you run into people from the block, like Patrick, all the time at the dry cleaner or the corner store. We've got to look for God to give us any opportunity to get His name into the heart of somebody who doesn't know Him. In the daily flow of missional living is missional engagement. If our prayer is Colossians 4, for God to open up the doors for opportunities for the Word, then just living in the community, being a good neighbor, sweeping up the front of the house, you just will naturally run into people. That was the case with Patrick.

PART 3

SPEAKING OF
(your city here)

*". . . and on this rock I will build
my church, and the gates of hell shall
not prevail against it."*

—MATTHEW 16:18

CHAPTER 9

FEAR

We all fear something. Fear in urban ministry often presents itself by hiding from the people or running from the difficulties. Our fear turns into excuses and creates barriers that prevent us from dynamically sharing the gospel and personally investing in the lives of our neighbors.

Fear of rejection was a primary insecurity for me. I was surprised by the number of brothers and sisters who felt they would mess up and stumble over their words when they shared their faith. They were embarrassed because they were not brilliantly theological, and they did not want to hinder anybody from meeting Christ because of their inability to communicate the gospel in the fullness of its majesty.

Another fear (closely related to that of rejection) common in my congregation was fear of failing to relate to people who were radically different from themselves. This was a particularly acute problem in my church at the time. The church was over one hundred years old and had seen its neighborhood transform from a largely white, thriving, working-class community to a violent, crime-ridden neighborhood with few white people at all. The

> **The challenges of the inner city seemed greater than God's reach.**

makeup of the church members, however, had largely not changed.

My congregation felt as though they were foreigners in their own neighborhood. Many of my older white members stated plainly that they could not share their story with people in the neighborhood because they did not feel as though they would be understood. Many noted their sense of cultural estrangement with statements such as, "I don't really get this new neighborhood."

They had a point. I realized my congregation was poorly equipped with antiquated missionary models. The African American and Latino kids could not relate to our ministry at all. The congregation was equipped with gospel engagement, but it was irrelevant to 95 percent of our neighborhood. In other words, the church had failed to equip them in such a way as to overcome these justified fears of distance and irrelevance.

As I probed these matters further with my congregation, I realized that the root of the fear was a collectively diminished view of the power of the gospel and the power of the church to spread it. My congregation lacked a God confidence in Christ's ability to reach lost people, no matter how difficult the context. The challenges of the inner city seemed greater than God's reach.

The lack of confidence in the power of the gospel and God's work through the church is positively toxic to proper missional engagement. Fears of rejection and irrelevance will stifle the spirits of your congregants. The church must equip its members for gospel engagement by emboldening them. We must pray passionately to combat this lack of faith, this lack of courage, this lack of *sentness*.

SPIRITUAL MEEKNESS

Proper missional engagement requires us to ask difficult questions of ourselves. I'll never forget listening to a pastor present a talk on missional engagement in 2007. He asked this question: "Are your covenant community members sharing the story of the faith in their relationships?" And I thought of a few members in my congregation that might describe. His next question was, "What percentage of your covenant community believes that telling these stories is tied to their mission for Christ?" That was a staggering and humbling question, and I could barely pay attention to the rest of the conference as I reflected on my pitiful answer.

I thought that line of questioning was intrusive yet penetrating, leading me to prayer and a Bible study series at my church on sharing your faith (which ultimately culminated in the completion of this book). It sparked a desire to search biblically for the most effective means of reaching the lost and equipping all the covenant community members of my local church to do the same.

I decided I should ask the same intrusive questions to my congregation: "Who believes that his or her story of coming to faith is tied to the mission of Christ?" To this, I added my own question: "Are we an army of missionaries growing together in our gospel engagement?"

That series of Bible study, book purchases, and refocused discipleship was instrumental in growing and developing our membership. We were immensely rewarded by God for our efforts. But it was a difficult time as well, requiring tough questions about the spiritual makeup of the congregation. As I came to see, the main spiritual lack was courage; the congregation was beset by a number of fears.

BARRIERS

There are several barriers to explore in order to understand and truly overcome the things that are keeping so many Christians from their block. Many of these barriers have to do with the way churches, institutions, and denominations have handled leaders on or en route to the urban context for ministry. I think many are well-intended, but sadly missing the mark of true support of missionaries, pastors, and church planters. It is my hope that we as Christ's church

> **Mission without movement never produces fruit.**

can repent and develop a whole reorientation for how we think and serve the Lord as partners to the inner-city context and not as power brokers. I pray that we as church leaders would simply just get out of God's way, submit to Him, and freely give, support, listen to, and fund leaders for the urban and inner-city context.

VISIONARY MANIPULATION

Pastoral manipulation is another barrier to missional engagement. When the leaders of the church spend their energy swooning their congregation with a big vision but do not act upon the vision themselves, they manipulate their congregation with a partial gospel that is false excitement without movement. The people will be all excited, but do nothing.

Mission without movement never produces fruit. Engaging in a missional conversation that does not lead to missional action is like having sex without marital commitment and fidelity. It's the difference between a one-night stand and starting a family.

There is no commitment to seeing the vision develop and mature. The congregation becomes addicted to the pastor as a personality instead of being led to the gospel of Jesus Christ and its missional implications.

The mission becomes an extension of the preacher's personality instead of being the gospel mission driven by Scripture. So often his great personality attracts Christians from other churches, and his church begins to grow numerically. These "church hoppers" simply take a leap out of one church and land in another. But numerical growth isn't spiritual growth. Having new people gives a false perception to the congregation that they are living missionally in their community.

Attractional becomes confused with missional. If it ever becomes a big personality preacher attracting fans of himself *instead* of shepherding followers of Jesus, that's when there is a problem. A follower of Jesus is someone who is marked by missional living, whose whole posture, behavior, and thinking is transformed by the gospel and the Great Commission being lived out in a lost and dying world. We must make Jesus the focal point of every decision, move, and life thought.

The result here, even if unintentional, is that the church begins to constrict itself. The church becomes more of a barbed wire fence than a swung open door. As we observed previously, they are "gathering" together, but not "scattering" with the gospel message.

In his book *The Gathered and Scattered Church*, Hugh Halter says something very interesting about this:

> I think the dilemma of church is really a dilemma of
> people. To put it simply I think it's an issue of spiritual
> formation. In some ways, I believe that even the gravity

toward consumerism is simply a symptom of how bored our people are with the basic Christian experience.[13]

Left to our own consumer-driven devices we have a low functional view of the vision and grace of God. We are completely underwhelmed by God's ability to transform lost people into active missionaries. We don't believe that every person can be equipped for relevant gospel engagement. Again, Halter says, "Our people just don't expect to see God do much anymore, and I'm not sure I do either." The pastor and elders are underwhelmed by God's *ability* and the congregation is overwhelmed by God's *inability*.

MISSIONAL DISCIPLES

We must make missional disciples! So how do we begin? The pastor must lead, teach, train, and seek to make missional disciples who will continually be surprised by grace and overwhelmed every time even one person is converted. The overwhelming reality of grace moves you from manipulation to celebration, from attractional to missional. It moves you from consumerism to calling on God to do a work beyond yourself. It moves you from calling people to the church building to calling them to Christ and the cross. It fundamentally changes how you view discipleship, and it will raise a whole new breed of urban missionaries who are effective, healthy, active, and missional, day in and day out seeking to share, spread, and serve people with the gospel.

ORGANIZATIONAL MANIPULATION

The pressures of organizations, quotas, and expectations can be a great burden to missional engagement in churches. The pressures of numerical and financial church growth that mission agencies, financial supporters, and denominations put on churches and church plants are often daunting, unrealistic, and intimidating. Church leaders often find themselves in the difficult spot of having to give a tangible account of the money they receive to do the ministry they have been called to.

Accountability and evaluation are critical and should be welcomed by pastors and church planters. But they must be accomplished in such a way as to drive the mission of the church. So often organizational pressure encourages church leaders to simply fill the seats with bodies who will show up, give a little money, and say amen from time to time when the picture is being taken for the newsletter instead of the hard work of making missional disciples and reaching the lost.

The vision to missionally engage the lost in the community in which God has called you is in danger of being reduced to simply filling out a progress report with inflated ideas about the Great Commission without actually living it out by faith in the gospel. Again, this begins to grow a non-gospel-centered, passive body of believers. They become complainers and are not committed. This is tragic for the lost, and harmful for the church.

We must learn that we can't call ourselves evangelical without being evangelistic. We must repent of calling church leaders to satisfy organizational quotas over and against seeing people satisfied with the Savior. This is a direct attack on the gospel that strains and restricts pastors and causes congregations to lose their missional vigor.

So how do we transition from snatching church hoppers to reaching lost people? Roland Allen in his landmark book, *The Spontaneous Expansion of the Church*, speaks about the spontaneity of believers' zeal for reaching the lost, which flows out of the Holy Spirit dwelling within them. I think that this aligns deeply with Jesus' words to the apostles in Matthew 28 and Acts 1:8. Obedience to Matthew 28 must impact each Christian, both those ordained as pastors as well as the person in the pew, to bring an active, intentional, and aggressive desire to reach lost people with the treasure of all ages: Jesus who is the Christ. Only then will people from all nations hear the gospel, respond to its call, and be converted. But what do we do after conversion?

Roland Allen says,

> We have not known how to expect it, we have not known how to deal with it, and consequently it is not rarer than it ought to be. Still it remains so essential, the natural action of that instinct to impart a joy, and that gift of the Holy Spirit, who is the spirit which desires and strives after the salvation of men, that in spite of our discouragement it constantly breaks out afresh.[14]

The urban missionary must not manipulate his flock or allow himself to be manipulated by denominations or sending agencies. Doing so creates a culture that is not passionate for lost people; it fosters pastoral manipulation to gather people to build his ego, and it leaves our churches staggeringly weak and incompetent to deal with the greatest need of a lost city.

Organizational pressures cause men to lead out of fear and not faith. That in turn causes fearful leaders to make fearful disciples. We must repent of our fear and, by God's grace, begin walking in faith. A. W. Tozer in *Of God and Men* sums it up: "Another characteristic of a true man of God is love. The free man who has learned to hear God's voice and dared to obey it has felt the moral burden that broke the hearts of the Old Testament prophets, crushed the soul of our Lord Jesus Christ and wrung streams of tears from the eyes of the apostles."[15]

CONTEXTUAL MISUNDERSTANDINGS

Often the inner-city context can be misunderstood due to a deep disconnect from many existing churches outside the inner city. This leaves incomplete understanding, uninformed ideas, and irrelevant ministry practices, which form a disheartening attitude toward urban missions.

I can remember being told by a white church that they don't plant African American churches, they plant white churches in white communities, and that's what God has taught and called them to do. These types of attitudes are formed because of the reductionistic and misinformed understanding of the Great Commission. Matthew 28:18 is a call to go to the nations (*ethnos*). The disciples would have understood that to mean all the unconverted people—every non-Jewish nation in the world—and baptize, pour your life into, and teach people to look like Jesus, act like Jesus, and bear the name of Jesus. This is a broad picture with wide coverage and far-reaching implications. That picture comes with the requirement to equip every member to live out the gospel so that the name of Jesus might be the most famous name. Yet, the context in inner cities can often drive outsiders away from seeking to engage the inner-city context with the gospel.

A lot of people view the city as too dangerous and too violent with no possible viability to establish or sustain a body of believers living missionally for Jesus. Often they would consider it too hard on their families and not worth the risk of danger, robbery, or death.

I don't want to sound like the angry black guy in the inner city, mad at the white church for not helping. I've heard African Americans have a posture against the city too. More than once I've heard some African American pastors comment, "They are too far gone," "They don't want to be bothered with the gospel," "They're not going to love Jesus," "You've got to find a place less dangerous that's more viable so you can get a paycheck," and "Get some people with fewer problems."

This leaves a gaping hole in new churches being planted in the inner cities. There's no real missional drive toward it other than the occasional mission trip. Those involved with such short-term investment turn the inner city into a spiritual petting zoo.

A pastor said to me once that he wanted his kids to come to Camden so they can see how good they have it in their suburban house, because they're always complaining that they don't have enough. I was on the verge of saying something that I would have needed to repent of. Instead, I told the man, "Don't bring your kids to the city to guilt them into feeling better about their own situation. Come for the call of the gospel, come to meet people changed by Jesus, come to serve the church in the city to reach the lost." He didn't like that very much, and he didn't end up coming. That's OK. My concern is when the masses don't come, when nobody finds it strange that the inner city is ignored, misunderstood, underdeveloped, unreached, and frankly, forsaken. We need a meeting of the minds, we need a summit, a conference, a dialogue where we can begin to clarify the confusion and pray to the Lord of the harvest. The harvest is plenty, and there's a deep need for missionaries to come to the inner cities of America with the gospel.

I get the privilege of serving on the board as vice president of Relational Connectivity for an organization I was a part of from its inception called Thriving. My pastor, Dr. Eric Mason serves as president. In 2010 we sought to contribute to the lack of inner-city leaders and churches on the block in the worst hoods in America. We have held multiple conferences yearly, and developed a residency program. Thriving partnered with Acts 29, The North American Mission Board, and Tenth Presbyterian Church, which was one of the first financial supporters of the conference. And what was birthed out of Thriving and the residency program is the planting of many churches in some of the most dangerous and poorest cities in America. However, the work is not done. We have a lot to learn and a long way to go. But God's hand seems to be upon the work to the block. Glory be to God!

* * *

A.W. Tozer makes a bold and courageous challenge and rebuke to men facing difficulties and barriers in ministry: "Each generation of Christians must look to its beliefs. While truth itself is unchanging, the minds of men are porous vessels out of which truth can leak and into which error may seep to dilute the truth they contain. The human heart is heretical by nature and runs to error as naturally as a garden to weeds. All a man, a church or a denomination needs to guarantee deterioration of doctrine is to take everything for granted and do nothing."[16]

What a statement. I need to hear that from time to time and truly that is a great challenge to the people serving on the blocks across the world.

If we're going to see exponential growth, we're going to need to greatly increase the number of teams led by blood-bought, Holy Spirit–filled missionaries who live out the gospel missionally, and seek to see the invisible church made visible through the preaching of the gospel.

CHAPTER 10

SUBMISSION

Submission to God's calling begins with a renewed emphasis on the great *urgency* of God's plan for the world.

Why is His plan urgent? It is urgent because the world is in dire need of it. We must constantly remind ourselves of that fact. We must constantly remind ourselves that we live in a world laced with hopelessness and overwhelmed by godlessness. It is a world of distraction, a world of deceit. More alarming still, it is a world beset by intentional attempts to pervert the church into being a contributor to this godlessness, or, at the very least, a passive recipient of grace that has no impact on its surroundings. Paul surely had these forces in his mind as he strenuously urged, commanded, pushed, and prodded Timothy to really absorb the impetus of his words.

In the context of this outlook, the Great Commission becomes a more focused command. I submit to you that when the church is not actively engaged in missional outreach, when it is not encouraging that outreach amongst all of its members, it must repent. After all, in the Great Commission we've been *promised* that Jesus would be with us always.

Let us not simply be ashamed by our failure to heed this command, but also be encouraged by it, because when the Lord has commanded something He will give us the grace to do it. We have the power, the Holy Spirit, and we have the message, the gospel!

The fact that we so often lack the sense of a holy urgency means in part that we have lost our sense of empowerment. We must remember our empowerment when we read that Jesus would have us pray to the Lord of the harvest (Matt. 9:38) that He might raise up harvesters. Why? Because *we* may very well be the answer to our own prayers.

We must develop Christ's motivations within ourselves—particularly His willingness to engage all types of people from various backgrounds (from a leper to a blind person, and from a Samaritan to a tax collector). We must have faith to believe that God is able to give us the courage to overcome our fears, our failures, and our lack of God-confidence. We must pray to Him earnestly and repent of this spirit of fear, and pursue the sound mind that Christ calls us to have as missionaries in the world.

I was fortunate to gain a glimpse of a church culture motivated by this urgency as a young man growing up in Christ Temple Baptist Church in Paterson, New Jersey. Right before Reverend Robinson would close each sermon Sunday after Sunday, he told us that we must be born again. He told us that without Christ we could not see God. He told us that true joy and forgiveness flow out of the precious blood of Jesus. He told us we must therefore accept Christ Jesus as personal Savior.

After saying these things, he would take his microphone off of the stand and remind the congregation of the fact that soon (and very soon) Jesus would return. We could not afford to be late. Today needed to be the day that we accept Christ. I can hear the choir joining in the message of urgency with that old song, "Don't let it be too late. Don't put it off, don't wait. Don't let it be too late to change your life and give it to Christ."

Every Sunday he made it his business to emphasize the urgency of receiving Christ as Savior. We couldn't leave that church without him saying, "The doors of the church are open. Come give your life to Jesus."

Now, some would find this in modern day challenging and maybe not the most effective means of missional engagement; however, I think the church has a lot to learn from Reverend Robinson. He wanted everybody to be saved. He wanted everyone he met to meet Jesus. And he wanted them to receive Him that very moment, because, as he would often say, "If you walk away now without accepting Christ and get hit by a car and die, you won't be in heaven, you'll be in hell."

Like Reverend Robinson, the church must remember and be motivated by the desperate need of a world without Christ, a world that thirsts for the hope of the gospel. It is a world that is at enmity with God, at war with God, unreconciled to God. The church must remember that when the children of this world die, they will go to a godless hell, where they'll be eternally separated from God. We must remember that this is the intractable future for those who do not receive Christ as Savior.

This is why I must strongly urge my brothers and sisters who have decided to put missions on the back burner in their churches to reconsider their position. The church cannot afford to wait until it considers itself "holy enough." It also cannot afford to only allow a certain portion of its congregation to do the task.

Instead, the church should, at the very forefront of its teaching, equip *all of* its members to develop what I call a "conversion hope intensity." The church must cause its congregation to feel heartbreak at the thought of the condemnation owed the wicked —grieving as God Himself grieves over sin (Ezekiel 33:11). And it must enliven its congregation's soul to fervently seek for the salvation of the wicked, acting with full confidence in the gospel. Finally, it must equip its congregation with tools for relevant gospel engagement and challenge their hearts to have a holy urgency. Darrell Guder sums it up like this: "Mission is not just a program of the church. It defines the church as God's sent people. Either we are defined by mission, or we reduce the scope of the gospel and the mandate of the church. Thus our challenge today is to move from church with mission to missional church."[17]

My friend and brother Matt Chandler serves as lead pastor of The Village Church in Texas. There is a statement on The Village Church's website that perfectly articulates my thoughts on missional living and that I find useful in many contexts:

> We want to be intentional about life, to live life on purpose. Acts 17:26 says that, "He (God) made from one man every nation of mankind to live on all the face of the earth, having determined their appointed times and the boundaries of their habitation. . . ." This means that God was intentional about our lives. He placed us in neighborhoods, work places, classrooms, gyms and coffee shops on purpose. Life is not a random accident; rather, God designed it with intention and purpose. We express missional living simply through obedience.
>
> We want to live the way of Jesus in front of the audience that God has given us. We love, serve and care for

those that God has "determined" us to be around in the hopes they will see Jesus in us, hear us speak of Him often and be drawn to Him. We extend our lives missionally when we introduce or re-introduce our neighbors, co-workers, family and friends to great and glorious gospel of Jesus Christ.

This mission statement reminds us of our call to live missionally in a hostile world. It also aligns with the Great Commission from Matthew 28:16–19, which is a direct command from Christ to His church to make disciples of all nations. In Acts 2, we see that the people who have come to Jesus from all over the world are being dispersed back to the cities and countries they originally came from. These people would go home and share this new faith they had received with others in their respective contexts; in essence, they would have lived missionally. The Great Commission would be lived out post the apostle Peter's great message in Acts 2. Missional living corresponds with the gospel, which demands our obedience. The Great Commission is not just an option for believers in Christ, but the basis of our mission. Thomas Hale Jr., missionary to the Himalayan Mountains in Nepal, put it like this:

> No one can say: "Since I'm not called to be a missionary, I do not have to evangelize my friends and neighbors." There is no difference, in spiritual terms, between a missionary witnessing in his home town and a missionary witnessing in Kathmandu, Nepal. We are all called to go—even if it is only to the next room, or the next block.[18]

When I talk about living missionally, I am referring to the believer in Christ responding to the mission of Jesus in the world by incarnating the gospel to the people they have been called to.

Like Jesus, we are called to jump into the culture and live in a way that expresses our faith in Him and points people to the Father in every way. Of course, this does require some contextualization. Missional living is different in every context. Whether we are in the suburbs with beautiful lawns and deep refreshing pools, or in a back alley in the streets of Detroit, we are to embody Jesus to a people who do not know Him. We should not simply tell people to "turn or burn." Rather, we are to share Jesus' message in John 3:17 that "God did not send his Son into the world to condemn the world, but in order that the world might be saved through him." We have come to dwell among the "people of the block" as we embrace ambassadorial living, or living our lives for Christ as His human message. We are to focus on connecting with people with the desire to connect them to Christ. In other words, we must declare the gospel both through our lives and our lips.

> **Many people see the church (both the building and the people) as an entity that is completely separated from their communities.**

Missional living calls us to translate the gospel through multiple outlets and cultural connectors. We can utilize resources such as movies, stories, life events, and news to show Jesus as the true and living God. Missional living tears down the imaginary walls that are all too real for many people in our neighborhoods. Many people see the church (both the building and the people) as an entity that is completely separated from their communities. These walls have grown thicker and thicker over the years to the people outside the membership of the church. In many neighborhoods, the local church carries the stigma that outsiders and residents of the surrounding community are not welcome. Our attitudes and actions have contributed to shaping how the church is viewed. We often leave the block out of the equation. It is not uncommon for churches to have buildings in neighborhoods where they simply do not care about their neighbors there.

Help us, Lord! We need Thee every hour! Missional living, then, calls churches to reengage in their communities as residents and neighbors, take on a missionary-like posture, and inhale the smells and absorb the sounds that make up the ethos of the block. This is a missional imperative. Jesus led the way in His life and ministry, and we are called to do the same in our churches. You can find prominent examples of missional living in the book of Acts, as the apostle Paul aggressively engages the known world for Christ. From its very inception, we can see that missional living is the norm for the first-century church.

In a certain sense, there is nothing particularly "urban" at the heart of urban ministry. Indeed, our efforts will be frustrated whenever we use preconceived, cultural expectations as our lens for gospel engagement, rather than using gospel engagement as the lens by which we set our cultural expectations. What matters most is that the church is emotionally engaged in the hurt and darkness of the context in which it finds itself and that it boldly proclaims the gospel into that context with an agonized, loving heart.

The crucial starting point for such a church is cultivating a heart that is passionate for individuals, and unhindered by cultural biases. One does not need to look far for an archetypal display of this heart. As we explored earlier, a naked, unrestrained passion for individual people was a fundamental aspect of Christ's ministry. Again and again, we see examples of Jesus' refusal to be constrained by cultural expectations or assumptions. Instead, Jesus gets up close and personal. He ministers to the *individual person*, He does not minister to them according to that person's rank or status.

The importance of having a passion for people is applicable in many contexts. Cultural hierarchies and statuses can be barriers. They create distance, separating us from each other on the basis of presumptions. Such presumptions allow us to think that we know why a person is hurting from afar, without ever engaging in a conversation with him or her. And yet, true love for all of God's creation calls us to defy such assumptions—to not miss the trees for the forest. This is acutely true in the urban context, in which the intensity of individual sufferings is heightened and the assumptions can create a particularly vast distance between the sufferer and the onlooker.

What does this look like in the struggling inner-city context? It means that the role of the church is far greater than we often think. If we are to provide for the whole of a person's suffering, then the presence of more suffering means there is more to be provided for.

First and foremost, interpersonal interaction is crucial. Our church has made it our priority to be a church that *talks* and *listens* to its community. We have strived to simply get to know the people around us. We want to know where their wants, needs, and sufferings are. This is the only way to ensure that we can tailor our care in an appropriate way.

This task places two requirements on us. First, we must *customize* our engagement to their particular cultural customs and language. In order to truly communicate with a community, one must speak in terms that it can understand. It is not unlike the difference between truly fluent speakers of a language and those who may know the basic terms but cannot express themselves as native speakers. If we do not speak to our communities with cultural fluency we will not be able to communicate, or worse, we will miscommunicate our message.

Second, our conversations must *avoid* all distracting cultural assumptions and barriers, so that we can see each person as an individual with the potential to be clothed in righteousness. From my experience in inner-city ministry, this has generally required churches to tear down norms and conditions that they have developed passively by virtue of living in a different context. In some instances, this division has been created *within* churches. This often happens when church membership is used as the sole determination as to whether one must show compassion to a given person to the exclusion of those who are regular attendees, but not members.

Finally, this approach requires more of a "Crock-Pot" approach to ministry rather than a "frying pan" approach. A Crock-Pot cooks food slowly. You simply put in the ingredients and check on it every now and again as all the seasonings and juices you put in work together over time to form one awesome result. The Crock-Pot retains the flavor of the ingredients because it is cooked slower. On the other hand, the frying pan cooks food quickly. It requires your constant attention, stirring, flipping, manipulating the food so it does not burn. While cooking in the frying pan the spices and flavors can easily evaporate into the air and be lost.

So it is with a healthy approach to missional engagement. We must reach people with a Crock-Pot, slow cook, philosophy as we patiently wait on the Lord to demonstrate His power. We present the gospel, but we do not coerce conversions. We teach the whole counsel of God slowly, allowing people to become saturated with the truths of God's Word. We seek radical and lasting change, not a flash in the pan. We heal the wounds we can, while presenting the gospel in a manner that allows its truly regenerating effect to be known (rather than in a manner that causes grace to feel like a blitzkrieg).

I should note that this metaphor only applies to interactions between the church and its community, not the behavior of the church itself. Inside the church, the metaphor works in reverse: when the church gathers together, the frying pan must *come out* and the Crock-Pot put away. It must pray without ceasing, fervently and energetically pleading with our God that His great gospel will be received. The church needs the constant searing heat that the gospel brings in the frying pan.

We also do not seek conversions merely for the outward shell of godless moralism. We cannot expect the immediate, total abdication of cultural practices that are sinful. We cannot demand that the new believer abandon or give away his entire collection of music, or immediately cease from using certain kinds of language. Rather, we must be willing to allow for progressive sanctification and recognize that there are certain cultural practices deeply imbedded into the people we are desiring to serve. This is where the balance of grace and patience is particularly required of us. God promises that His Spirit will transform people, but never are we told it will be instantaneous or that we must first change our behavior before coming to Christ.

In my opinion, the key theological application of this biblical model is a thorough reliance on the work of the Holy Spirit.

We are, after all, merely carrying out a plan with an outcome that has been sealed from the beginning. I believe we find an underlying irony behind every book on missional engagement: the more broadly they describe the people, culture, and problems, and the more concrete and specific the method, the less helpful it is. Why? Because every broad statement misses the uniqueness of each community. With every rule, we threaten to confine the power of the Holy Spirit. With every projection, we set ourselves up to be embarrassed by God's sovereign creativity.

After all, we serve a God who created something out of nothing . . . who made dry land appear in the middle of the sea, and whose story of redemption was predesigned to defy every expectation. The one who descended to become at once fully man and fully God. He took on the form of a servant and paradoxically died a humiliating death as His stroke of victory. Therefore we must not go first to the lesson books! Consider throwing away the mission maps! We must first learn to be utterly reliant upon God through a full awareness of His complete sovereignty. We must be constantly in the Word, constantly in prayer, and constantly prepared to be surprised by God's plan for our ministry in our unique situation.

In *The Mission of God: Unlocking the Bible's Grand Narrative*, Christopher Wright encapsulates the sound theological truths that underlie the radical reliance on God I am advocating. As he notes, that mission is not ours; the mission is God's. Certainly, the mission of God is the prior reality out of which flows any mission we get involved in. Or, as has been nicely put, it is not so much the case that God has a mission for His church in the world but that God has a church for His mission in the world. Mission was not made for the church; the church was made for mission . . . God's mission.

Cities like mine are inherently dark, chaotic places. Senseless murder, drug abuse, prostitution, abortions, and abuse on every corner. Satan and his forces have taken a firm grip, and his servants are many. When we bring light into the darkest of places, we have to be ready for attacks from every angle. Satan appears to have every vantage point covered, and he will use each and every one of them to thwart God's purposes and the church's efforts.

In the face of such a multiplicity of dark forces, the church must be ready for the radical manner in which God's light will burst forth. In the face of desperate need, God's grace and power will be shown in mighty and sudden ways. For every demonstration of God's power on the grandest scale, there will be just as many moments of equally astonishing displays on the smallest and quietest of scales. God's power will be present in quiet moments as well as the loud.

It is only by God's story that the plot will progress.

Finally, we must be dependent on God for His practical provisions. An urban church is frequently not self-sustaining. When most of its members are making less than $50,000 a year (and often much less), it cannot rely on weekly tithes and offerings to provide all the finances needed. I admit the question, "How are we going to *pay* for this?" is ringing in my ears constantly. The urban church finds itself in a place much like that of the nation of Israel in the book of Exodus. It is in constant need of daily manna from heaven, and it owes God its constant prayer, seeking and thanking Him for His provision.

This should help demonstrate why a legalistic approach to urban missions proves to be so problematic. When we set up preconceived notions for how God ought to work, we attempt (despite often having the right intentions) to control the manner in which God can spread His gospel. We seek authority over His plan; we want to write our own narrative. Considering what was just mentioned, note that we must do the exact opposite. It is only by God's story that the plot will progress. Any other path is one of futility, because it seeks to contain One who is without boundaries.

I hope it's clear that this is not simply a theological point—it is a highly practical point. We, quite literally, cannot afford to write our own blueprint for building a church. Far be it from me, then, to write a book that will provide you a step-by-step outline to building a church. The first step to engaging in urban missions is to realize that there are no "steps." In what follows, I hope to provide nothing more than humble guidance and anecdotes. I do not intend to provide the blueprint to the "perfect urban church." Instead, I pray that I will be able to help illustrate an example of what the heart of an urban missionary looks like, so that the reader will develop a similar heart. I aim to equip the urban missionary so that he is ready to carry out his own unique ministry in his own unique context. Actually, I should say *God's* unique ministry for you in your unique circumstance.

CHAPTER 11

SENTNESS

"And he gave the apostles, the prophets, the evangelists, the shepherds and the teachers, to equip the saints for the work of ministry, for building up the body of Christ, until we all attain to the unity of the faith and of the knowledge of the Son of God, to mature manhood, to the measure of the stature of the fullness of Christ." (Ephesians 4:11–13)

"You then, my child, be strengthened by the grace that is in Christ Jesus, and what you have heard from me in the presence of many witnesses entrust to faithful men who will be able to teach others also." (2 Timothy 2:1–2)

We, the church, have lost our sense of sentness. It is very, very important for the church to recognize that reaching the lost with the gospel is not a trendy idea for church growth, but a biblical mandate that every Christian is called to live out daily in honor to Christ. The loss of our sentness exposes the fact that we have not taken ownership of the lost state of our cities.

I define sentness as "the God-given mandate and Holy

Ghost–powered lifestyle of intentional, aggressive, prayer-bathed, missional engagement that embraces the biblical mandate to live out the gospel of grace in a hostile world."

The word *sentness*, of course, is not necessarily found in Scripture, but the biblical principles that make up my understanding are clearly in God's Word. When I say I feel that the church has lost its sense of sentness, it's as if we've lost our apostolic impulse. Though we don't believe in the continuation of the office of apostle, we believe that the apostolic impulse should be common to every believer, and should drive us to take the gospel to a lost world with ownership and passion as dictated to us by the Great Commission.

The neighborhood church on the block must refocus and embrace the mission of the gospel and own our God-given sentness. Several years ago, Dr. Ken Purdy got me thinking along the lines of the church refocusing and reclaiming its sense of sentness. Ken's ministry pertains to church revitalization and yet for the purposes of this book, many of his principles are also applicable for the church's revitalization of missional engagement of America's unreached neighborhoods and people groups.

Often young churches start out very people-driven, desiring to engage every aspect of human life in their target area. They often interact with the community around them through local schools, Boy Scout meetings, and multiple civic organizations, all for the purpose of reaching the whole community with the gospel. When young church-plant teams go into cities and purchase homes to move into neighborhoods, they're having cookouts, dinner parties, and Super Bowl parties all for the purpose of getting to know the neighbors. This is the embracing of our God-given sentness to the world. This is the greater church embracing our Great Commission mandate for the sake of the sender, Jesus.

Many people on core teams spend a great amount of time, energy, and prayer on the people they meet in their daily lives. They invest in the network of relationships they're developing through work, family activities, and social outings (i.e., movies, dinners, cookouts, etc.). Simply put, most people involved with young church plants often utilize every relational component and opportunity to engage people in their lives, from the dry cleaning lady to the manager at the Chick-fil-A. Sentness also expresses itself as a pursuit of praying for God-given opportunities to lead someone to Jesus.

Early on in the young church plant there is a passion for people. Dr. Ken Purdy would call this the "church on the incline." The church on the incline is people-driven, gospel-focused, and has a deep desire to see many and any come to the saving knowledge of Jesus. They're willing to put their lives on the line for the mission of the gospel. However, what can begin to happen to the young church plant is a loss of that passion and vigor for people over time.

This problem often happens post-launch of the church plant after there's been significant growth: baptisms, packed-out new-member class sessions, and a sense of the neighborhood's acceptance of the new church in the community. Now that your church has a host of new people, believers and nonbelievers, it is flirting with adding a second worship service. The leaders now feel compelled to move from mission and ministry to simply managing the existing congregation. They've transitioned from a vibrant, gospel-centered, people-driven community of faith to a program-driven group of Christians. If the people-driven church is the church on the incline, then Ken Purdy would say that the program-driven church is the church on the recline.

For the young vigorous church on the incline, it's as if they were pursuing a sort of missional nirvana. As young missionaries to cities, we must understand that people are not a means for pastors to build and establish a platform for them to preach to. People need Jesus, not just another pastor with privilege and title—a parking spot at a large church, with no visible presence in the *restoration* of the city. Lost people are not the building blocks for a preaching platform. Often when we've lost our sense of sentness, we see the lost residents of our city as projects and not people, when in fact they are a lifelong mission assignment for the church on the block. Missional engagement is not to be a temporary action for the purposes of establishing a ministry and securing a job—may it never be. Missional engagement is a lifelong discipline for the Christian.

Why does this happen? Why is there a loss of sentness in our churches? One of the key reasons this happens and continues to happen across the nation is because of what I believe to be a discipleship issue. J R Woodward challenges the church to see the comprehensive work of the congregation of mission being more than just an afterthought. He says, "Creating a missional culture is more than just adding some outward programs to the church structure. Creating a missional culture goes to the heart and identity of God, to who we are and who we are becoming."[19] In other words: we may need to tear down the building and rebuild, not just paint and clean up a little.

My good friend Pastor Chris Atwell of Portico Church says, "The church is always sent and never settled." What a great and profound statement. When there is a deep sense of sentness in the soul of the missionary to the city, Christ's mission prevails over achieving a type of ministry nirvana. What I mean by that is: after a good season where the Lord has used you and your church to bring people to Christ, we can far too easily move from a church that has a deep passion for reaching the lost in our neighborhoods to the church that is program-driven and is settled because of complacency. Sentness is at the heart of Jesus' redemptive work to the lost world.

> **Sentness is at the heart of Jesus' redemptive work to the lost world.**

In Mike Shamy and Jim Petersen's book about evangelism, *The Insider*, they state that

> Jesus was the first apostle. He was sent by His Father. He, in turn, sent the Twelve. They went to people who would then take the gospel to the rest of the world. Whoever received it would understand that they, too, had been sent. With the gospel being what it is, the church as bearer of the gospel is bound to be apostolic.[20]

In Isaiah 6:8 we see Isaiah's response to God's general call to mission and obedience. "And I heard the voice of the Lord saying, 'Whom shall I send and who will go for us?' Then I said, 'Here am I! Send me.'" This is the picture of sentness—Isaiah's response to God upon receiving the work of atonement in his life. He has been transformed and refocused. King Uzziah has died, and Isaiah is seeing God anew through transformed eyes. Having had a seemingly near-death experience at seeing the glory of God's presence fill the temple, Isaiah is now focused on serving God fully, even before he receives the assignment (which is a rugged one) to go and serve God on a mission. He's seen the Lord high and lifted up, God has atoned for his sins, and he is consumed by God's grace. He responds by crying out to the Lord, "Here I am Lord, send me." Eric Hesse says, "Isaiah became missional because of grace. Herein lies the sentness principle. The greater the internal gratitude, the greater the missionary impulse in a person's life."[21]

John 20:21 is another beautiful picture of sentness in the context of community. It reads, "Jesus said to them again, 'Peace be with you. As the Father has sent me, even so I am sending you.'" John records here Jesus' declarative statement of reaching the world through obedience to the Father. Jesus is making a direct connection between the sentness of the church to the Father's sending of His own Son. The Father had sent Jesus into the world, a hostile place that He knew would crucify and murder Him brutally on the cross, and yet He came knowingly amongst us (John 1:4). So as Jesus reflected the Father's glory in a dark world, willfully going to the dark crevices of the earth, taking the light of the gospel and obeying the will of God, His sender, so should we be to the world around us. This idea that we are called to imitate God's missional heart has a theological richness that profoundly displays sentness.

We must keep in mind that sentness is a path, not an achievement. The church is always to live as those who are sent: to go forth, accomplish God's commission, and bring Him glory. We are never to shrink back from going to a dark world and embracing the sentness given to us through the Holy Spirit and commissioned to us from this beautiful verse in John 20:21. The church is to be the living embodiment of the work of Christ. We are to continue what Jesus began to do and to teach, whether it be on the farm on the country road, on the highway in the suburbs, or on the violent block in the inner cities of America. We are to walk in the transformational power of God as we live out the gospel—engaging, growing, and developing as sent ones. This is the mandate. This is the mission.

Through the church, God makes Christ's invisible kingdom tangible in every region and sphere of life: spiritually, socially, and culturally. This is the embracing of sentness. This is what our Sender, Jesus, has called us to.

I stated that our lost sense of sentness is a discipleship issue. We must remember what we've been sent to do. At Epiphany Church, we call it "the five Ms": meet, make, mature, multiply, and mobilize disciples to engage a lost world with the gospel of Jesus.

God has not called us to be *nice* people, but *new* people.

The church is essentially a community of disciple-making disciples. These disciples must be made and matured with the intent to be missional as God commands. The church that desires to send others must have a clear plan and pathway for this type of engagement and discipleship. Isaiah 6 and John 20 are rich with this sentness impulse that believers ought to have. Often discipleship can take the form in our churches of a Christian etiquette course, where young believers are taught how to be nice, but God has not called us to be *nice* people, but *new* people. That newness should be loaded with the reality of our sentness.

Meet

From the cookout we have on the Fourth of July to our trip to the dry cleaners, we're constantly meeting people, inviting them into our personal lives, the lives of the church, and sharing the life of Jesus with them.

Make

Through our meeting with others, many come to be converted, embrace the gospel, and walk in the newness of life. That's the idea of making disciples through evangelism and missional engagement. This is directly tied to the Great Commission (Matt. 28:16–19). God has commissioned us and sent us into the world to make disciples of all nations, baptizing them, and teaching them all that Christ commanded. The process of making disciples is seeing young believers that we've met grow from spiritual infancy to spiritual maturity.

Mature

This maturing aspect comes with the regular flow of living together in community. This maturing carries with it an idea of discipleship, mentoring, teaching, and growing young converts into more mature believers through life-on-life coaching and regular connection and contact (Acts 2:42).

Multiply

Second Timothy 2:2 boldly says, "And what you have heard from me in the presence of many witnesses entrust to faithful men who will be able to teach others also." Paul tells Timothy that as he's been entrusted with spreading the gospel, through divine means, not through human invention, Timothy is to deposit what he's heard from many witnesses into faithful men, because they are the ones who are going to reach the continued generations.

Mobilize

We don't multiply disciples just for the sake of filling the room. They're multiplied that they might be mobilized and sent into a lost world with the gospel of Jesus. Mobilization is the heart of sentness. This is the discipleship component that can be missing in our churches. A lot of pastors have a reductionist view of sentness, because they've never experienced it through discipleship themselves, and often the church can get caught in building a kingdom in one place, as opposed to the mobilization of mature disciples dispatched to the lost cities in our country. In Acts 13:2–3, some prophets and teachers had been worshiping and fasting before the Lord, and the Holy Spirit spoke to them these words, "'Set apart for me Barnabas and Saul for the work to which I have called them.' Then after fasting and praying, they laid their hands on them and sent them off."

Christopher Wright makes it clear that he sees the whole Bible as a missional Magna Carta: "The Bible is the drama of this God of purpose engaged in the mission of achieving that purpose universally, embracing past, present and future, Israel and the nations, 'life, the universe and everything,' and with its center, focus, climax, and completion in Jesus Christ. Mission is not just one of a list of things that the Bible happens to talk about, only a bit more urgently than some. Mission is, in that much-abused phrase, 'what it's all about.'"[22]

If believers are to live "sent lives," we must see biblically that God has sent His Son, and His Son, Jesus, is sending His church. Furthermore, we see this sending of Christ's church as fully interwoven into all that we are and do as Christians.

We must, as Christopher Wright explains, not see mission as just an item on the to-do list but as the core of what the Bible is about. Therefore, sentness must be laced into the regular outworking of our discipleship so that at every point of our missional engagement—meeting, making, maturing, multiplying, and mobilizing disciples of Christ—sentness is a natural and beautiful by-product.

As church planters, we can never lose sight of the truth that we want to see people converted to Christ in our city. We call people to repentance, preach sound doctrine, shepherd the broken, and use anointing oil to pray over the sick. We're on the block; we recognize the weight of people not knowing Jesus Christ every day in our physical reality. We recognize the implications of the godlessness in our cities, such as record-breaking rates of abortion, illiteracy, unemployment, and homelessness. We've been called, challenged, and commissioned to step into the absence of God to proclaim the God of heaven and His Son Jesus Christ as the present hope in times of trouble—the true redeeming presence of all things good.

LEARNING YOUR BLOCK

The importance of knowing the idiosyncrasies of a particular community when engaging in gospel missions is also clearly demonstrated by Paul's ministry. When speaking with the Greeks at the Areopagus, Paul sought to evangelize the philosophers of the day in a manner that engaged the unique concerns of his listeners. For example, he understood the value they placed on philosophical dialogue and the existence of gods. He used analogies from their poetry as well as from their altar to the "unknown god" to point them to Christ. In so doing, he engaged in missions in a manner that was utterly distinct from the manner in which he engaged the Jews.

Following the examples clearly set forth in the Scriptures, we who seek to engage our cities and neighborhoods must thoroughly learn our cities and neighborhoods. We must learn our community's language, its local values and beliefs, its art, its habits, its food, and its history. These aspects of a place's identity are not simply useful tools by which the gospel can be proclaimed; they provide the avenues by which an agonized mission is carried out. It is only by understanding a particular setting that one can fully understand its needs and its pain. By learning the culture, one comes to view the world through its perspective. Only from that vantage point can an urban missionary truly understand a community's wants and needs and feel and empathize with its pain. Only if he is armed with that perspective will he be able to apply the gospel in a manner that is powerful and life-shattering.

Without such armament, the gospel will be hindered. For example, if we do not speak the language of the culture, the culture will not understand our words, no matter how majestic. If we do not know the history of the culture, we will have trouble connecting the truths of the gospel and the story of Christ's great redemptive plan to the individual stories of the city's residents. If we do not know the city's art, we lose insight into the imagination of its members and the manner in which it seeks to reach for something higher. We therefore lose important means for powerfully displaying the majesty of God.

Paul Hiebert notes this best when discussing the duty of a missionary in his book *Understanding Folk Religion*: "Missionaries must cross linguistic, cultural, and social boundaries to proclaim the gospel in new settings. They must translate and communicate the Bible in the languages of people in other cultures so that it speaks to them in the particularities of their lives. They must bridge between divine revelation and human contexts, and provide biblical answers to the confusing problems of everyday life."[23]

This is why Dr. Eric Mason's church, Epiphany Philadelphia, provides a course titled, "Exegeting the City." Whether or not a formal class is feasible in every context, I wholly support the spirit behind it. We as the church must engage in a close study of a city's culture, i.e., its shared understanding of itself, the world, and its place therein—in order to ensure that the gospel has its deepest and most powerful impact.

And once we have come to understand our neighborhood, it is crucial that we use what we have learned to actually speak the language. This does not mean changing the gospel—far be it from me to suggest such blasphemy! Instead, we must maintain biblical truth, using a language that our neighbors can understand. As Ed Stetzer notes in his work *Planting Missional Churches*, in order for a church to be truly *missional*, it must be "learning and adapting to the culture around [it] while remaining biblically sound."[24]

At my church, we are placed in a distinctly urban context. Accordingly, we have tried to imbue the gospel into the urban culture, to allow it to speak most effectively to the people of Camden. Those who have heard our podcasts will surely have noticed that we speak the language in our sermons, utilizing whatever analogies we can find. For example, we titled our sermon series working through the gospel of Mark as "Jesus on His Grind," using language that will evoke strong imagery of the relentless, daily efforts our Savior undertook to bring redemption to His people. Within our sermons, we use local metaphors wherever we can. So we might say that we're not worthy to untie Jesus' "Jordans" (referring to Michael Jordan's sneaker line), rather than his "sandals" or "shoes."

I have also embraced what might to others appear to be a

shocking informality, permitting myself to be called "Diddy." In Camden, the use of nicknames is a means by which a community comes to embrace a newcomer. It is a term of affection, and creates a sense of familiarity and intimacy where there previously had been none. When I first moved to Camden, I made it a point to meet as many people as I could. Although at first I introduced myself as Pastor Doug, I noticed that the name quickly changed. I soon became "Pastor D," then "PD," then "P. Diddy." My name has seemingly settled now on simply "Diddy." I have not fought this transformation of my name, nor have I insisted on being addressed according to my title. I know that such an insistence would only create distance between me and those I am trying to reach. It would amount to an extreme failure to understand the cultural significance of nicknames. To the contrary, I have embraced my new name, and will continue to embrace whatever future iterations present themselves.

Our church's customs and practices cater to the needs of our community. For example, we don't expect our congregation to wear fancy outfits, knowing that far too many would be unable to afford such clothes. Our first-Sunday fellowship meals are barbecues (rather than more formal, sit-down meals) as often as weather permits. What we are trying to do is bring the worship of Christ to terms that are accessible and familiar to the folks we're serving.

We also infuse our worship with urban arts. Instead of music from organs and classical instruments, our hymns are often mixed with the colors of jazz and soul. Rather than reciting stanzas, we often follow a more call-and-response format to our worship. And at our barbecues and fellowship meals, we usually have hip-hop music playing in the background, preferring the musical stylings of Lecrae and Propaganda.

Let the culture be our outline for our sermon, and as long as we do solid biblical exegesis with the backdrop of the culture, I think people will be able to let their hair down and hear. People on my block had never seen a pastor in a Polo and Timberlands before, never seen one joking, breeding dogs, wearing hoodies, listening to Mobb Deep—they'd just not seen that before. And so by the time I start talking with them, their typical resistance is down, that is, their knee-jerk rejection and the first thing they want to say to a preacher is, "You don't understand the block." When people on my block learn that I'm from Paterson, New Jersey, and that I was born and raised in the hood, on a block just like their own, there seems to be a disarming element that the Lord uses to connect me with my neighbors. People on my block, though, come to know that I'm a street joker with them, and not a thug. I'm just from the street. Big difference. And they know the difference. Coming from the street, I know the difference between a .45 and a .22. I know the difference between a real Jordan and a fake one from the local flea market. I know that. I know a lot of stuff from the street. So when people get that I understand the block, and they let their hair down, and they want to know what's good, I tell them, "You need to be with Jesus. You and Jesus are beefin' right now. Listen. Jesus ain't ever lost a beef. Ever. So I'm saying Jesus is looking for progress, not perfection."

We do not compromise the gospel or its demands. It is my prayer that those who listen to our podcasts can clearly see Christ and His work alone proclaimed. I remain entirely wedded to the text and its proper exegesis. I have tried to ensure this meaning is packaged in a manner that is readily accessible and most poignant to my church, in order that they may receive the gospel in a manner unadulterated by translation issues.

A CLOSER INSPECTION ON "CULTURAL SENSITIVITY"

Much of what I have touched upon in this chapter relates to the question of cultural sensitivity. In other words, the importance of understanding and knowing the culture one enters while spreading the gospel.

We must fully immerse ourselves into the city's darkness. We will rub up against fatherlessness and felony charges of our congregants. We will be called on to break up fights, and give cash for bus rides to court appearances. We will find ourselves stepping into drug transactions, and into rooms filled with weed smoke and angry, violent arguments. We must always beware of the potential to be robbed at gun- or knife-point while sharing the gospel. We run the risk of getting caught in the cross fire of a shoot-out. While serving in the city, we will come across high levels of illiteracy with children who live there. We even run the risk of being called a snitch because we live as law-abiding citizens.

We must remember that in many cases grace, redemption, and justification don't carry the same meaning. Many of our Christian terms carry the idea of legal terms affiliated with their sense of struggle and abandonment. A *grace* period is related to payment on bills that are way past due. *Redemption* is related to the ticket you get from the pawn shop as you have pawned your valuables to survive in the city. And *justification* is connected to what we hear from lawyers in reference to assault and murder charges.

As believers with a desire to reach the city we must come to the neighborhood with these realities as a presupposition and as a cultural foundation to work from. However, as we engage the city with a cultural sensitivity, we must remain gospel-centered, consistently making Christ the center rather than the cultural concerns becoming paramount. We cannot step in simply to put forth our theological arguments against the culture, using people to flesh out whatever new theological book we have been reading or studying for seminary. We must remember that many of our deep theological thoughts are foreign language for an initial conversation. John and Calvin are drug dealers on my block. The only "Martin Luther" they know is not a German monk, but someone whose last name is King. Therefore, we must engage the city with a relevant reality that clearly presents Jesus as King and Lord. And God's Word as eternally relevant. We must keep in mind that the gospel we share and preach is full of hope! The block is often full of hopelessness; therefore, we must be hope hustlers. G. K. Chesterton said,

> Hope means hoping when things are hopeless, or it is no virtue at all. . . . As long as matters are really hopeful, hope is mere flattery or platitude; it is only when everything is hopeless that hope begins to be a strength.[25]

When we step into the culture without a real cultural sensitivity, having prayed for words "seasoned with salt" (Col. 4:6), we do violent harm to perpetuate a cold, irrelevant church that is not in tune with the realities of the struggle of the block. We are called to be gospel-centered, hope-hustling, blood-washed, intentional and aggressive, Christ-preaching, city-reaching missionaries. And to do that, we have a prayer-bathed cultural sensitivity.

People have been insulated, isolated, and ostracized from the promises of God. We are on a rescue mission, not a recruiting mission. Rescue and recruiting are considered one thing in the gospel. As the Lord saves us, we are automatically called into

Christ's community, commitment to Christ, and commitment to the Great Commission. Jesus' gospel is for the streets. It's designed for the whole world and it certainly is for transforming cities. In reference to evangelism, one of my heroes in the faith, Dr. William Krispin, once told me,

> The people are out on the block, unsaved and unreached. The new planters and church leaders are not yet saved and they are out there on the block. But too many preachers are stuck inside the church cemented to the ground behind their pulpits. Doug, your pulpit has to have wheels on it to roll out the gospel of grace to those who are lost out on the block.

GOAL: AN INCESSANTLY PROACTIVE, CULTURALLY SENSITIVE BODY

In order to do this, it's time to revive our sense of *sentness*. As Christians, we have all been sent by God to go into our own city and communities as missionaries. Every believer is on a mission from God. We must be reminded of our identity as those sent by God (John 20:21). We must recognize the reality of the missionary commissioning that we received from Jesus in Matthew 28, John 20, and Acts 1. We need to be serious and aggressive in our missional obligation by living *sent* lives to the glory of Christ.

In 2 Corinthians 5:20 Paul calls us *ambassadors for Christ*. The *International Commentary on the New Testament* defines "ambassador" as one who "acts and speaks not only on behalf of, but also in the place of the sovereign from whom he has received his commission."[26] We have all received a commission from the Most

High God to be His ambassadors, to act and speak on His behalf and in His place, "as though He were making an appeal through us" (NASB).

Conversely, by having lost our sense of sentness, we have in some ways lost our sense of our calling. We have failed to take ownership of our roles as beacons of light in the darkness of our cities, neighborhoods, and communities. We have failed to be motivated as Paul was to reach the least, the last, and the lost in our cities. For this, my brothers and sisters, we must repent.

This was well understood by our Christian forebears, as Heinrich Kasting noted by saying, "Mission was, in the early stages, more than a mere function; it was a fundamental expression of the life of the church. The beginnings of a missionary theology are therefore also the beginnings of Christian theology as such."[27] Let us be motivated by their example!

The entire church must engage in gospel ministry. The gospel is not meant simply to be shared among the church's members, but it must extend, through those members, to the least, the last, and the lost. In short the church's mission is to transform the whole world—not just the members within its walls. Moreover, by engaging the world with the gospel, our members themselves grow in their sanctification.

The image of the spirit of the church is motion. We see an incessant hive of missional engagement. Each member is motivated to engage his community; each member is moving into his community to make sure it receives that engagement. And these characteristics are of utmost importance for a church that's on the block, surrounded by darkness. There's only one direction: outward. The church must be fully engaged in its community in order to fully reach that community. And yet, so many of our churches have failed to properly take on this mission.

SEPARATING HOLY LIVING FROM MISSIONAL LIVING

I remember being at a church planters meeting, during the course of which a conversation about missional engagement within the context of the initial church plant came up. There were people from various denominational traditions, many of whom believed that missional engagement was a matter to be delayed until the church's members were sufficiently holy. When the topic was specifically raised by the discussion leader, one of the young pastors stood up and said, "I don't agree with the missional movement. Though many passages in the Bible call us to be missional, there are far more that call us to be holy."

Another pastor responded to his statement by saying to the young man, "There is not a competition between missional living and holy living, nor are they opposite ends of the spectrum. After all, the Bible itself is a manifestation of God's mission to the world. Moreover, Christ Himself is the greatest missionary of the Bible, and yet He was surely holy. Missional living is one aspect of holy living!" And I totally agreed!

Unfortunately, some churches have come to see missional engagement as something to be delayed or limited to certain members. Such churches have decided that only some of its members have the particular qualities, gifting, and/or spiritual maturity. Other churches have decided that no missional engagement at all may occur until the church in its entirety has reached a level of spiritual maturity.

This strict separation between sanctification and missional living will hinder efforts of the church to properly equip its members. Rather, the church's missional engagement is one *means* of their sanctification. Therefore, the church must not wait for equipping its members. Promoting missional engagement is a means of shepherding the flock. It should be a pressing and active concern, not a matter to be avoided or considered tangential to the church's ministry.

Proactive missional engagement should also be the church's aim for all of its members. It should not be considered something for only those members with particular qualities, gifting, or spiritual maturity. Though it is certainly good to have "mission teams" and/or leaders who can organize, spearhead, and train the church body, these members should not be the exclusive means by which the church engages in missions. To allow this would be to deprive members of a crucial means of spiritual growth.

CHAPTER 12

DOING SOMETHING

Now we move to the final step in missional engagement—*taking action*. In a certain sense what I have said thus far should lead us to this point. In order to engage in missions we must be worshipful, develop a passion for people, learn about our communities, foster a spirit within our churches for missional living, and figure out how to communicate the gospel in a culturally relevant manner. All these things we must do in order that we might then *go forth* and do the work of bringing the lost to the light.

URBAN MISSIONS AS A HIVE OF ACTIVITY

If we are going to engage our communities missionally, we cannot expect the community to come into our walls. Instead we *go out* into those communities—not only to learn from them personally, but to engage them missionally. Moreover, this engagement is an outward movement that is diverse in its approach and direction. In other words, the church must be willing to enter into communities at multiple access points, using whatever opportunities to spread the gospel that present themselves.

Our model is in part influenced by the spirit of the early church. Paul's actions in the Acropolis were not a unique, one-time event. Indeed we find incessant activity throughout Paul's ministry. Consider also Acts 14, detailing the ministry of Paul and Barnabas in Greece. Particularly notable in their ministry is its momentum and diversity. Paul enters a Jewish synagogue in Iconium (Acts 14:1). He miraculously heals a random individual simply sitting on the street in Lystra (Acts 14:8–10). Immediately thereafter, he preaches a sermon to all those present when he senses they have associated him and Barnabas with false Greek deities (Acts 14:11–18).

> **They were prepared to preach that gospel by whatever means were appropriate to the context.**

So the ministry of Paul and Barnabas was filled with incessant activity. Moreover, they sought to preach the gospel wherever and whenever the opportunity presented itself. Their sermons were tailor-made to the circumstances, depending on their audience. They were conversant with both the Greeks and the Jews. They spoke to crowds *and* individuals. Moreover, they did not always see fit to "preach," but also demonstrated the power of the gospel through miraculous signs. In short, Paul and Barnabas went out, seeking every possible opportunity to preach the gospel that was presented to them, and they were prepared to preach that gospel by whatever means were appropriate to the context.

So must be our missions in the urban setting. We must have multiple access points, ready for whatever opportunity presents itself for the gospel light to shine forth. This, by the way, is why it is so important to *learn your block*. The better you learn the history, culture, and arts of your community, the more means you will have to communicate the gospel, and the more opportunities you will have to witness the Holy Spirit working miracles.

A ministry that is conjured up through mere abstractions and philosophies within church offices, unaffected and uninfluenced by the rhythm and beat of the block, will stifle the spread of the gospel in at least two ways. First, especially in the urban context, such ruminations tend to lead to a certain cultural narrow-mindedness. The church develops preconceived notions of who they should seek, and who they can engage. It will be confused by the bizarre speech of the block; it will recoil at its slang, its low-hanging jeans, its backward hats. In short, it will cast an artificially small net.

Second, a ministry that waits for the community to come into the church walls in order to start evangelizing will likely fail to produce much fruit. You see, corrupt churches have long been a source of suffering in the city. They are not so much "churches" of course, but cults of personality, which offer the veneer of truth and intoxicating lies of "prosperity." These churches swindle and rob their congregations, leaving them broken, confused, and mistrustful of all churches and pastors.

People who have been broken in this way will not enter church buildings of their own accord. We cannot simply wait for them to sit in our pews to teach them the love of Christ. Instead the church is to go out and reach the "ecclesiologically disconnected," as I call them, to teach them what the love of Christ in community *really* looks like. The church must break down those walls they have built up due to past experience in order to bring them into its own walls.

When our church first began in Camden we met in my back-yard, so we couldn't engage in a four-wall ministry if we tried! Our services were completely open. We played good music, preached passionately, and made sure there was food on the grill afterward. Each service was a natural act of community engagement.

One day, I noticed a lady outside the fence who was just listening to our service and crying. Her niece had just had a stillborn baby. She had been there, watching her poor niece give birth to a dead baby. I walked over to her, inviting her in, but she said she wasn't ready to come to church—having been disconnected from it for years. She sensed she just needed to hear some good news from God. About a month later, she became a regular attendee. Four years later, she received Christ and is now an active member.

A church that waits for communities to come into it, that has a sedentary gospel, will not reach people like this—quietly suffering and in need of the gospel, but wary of church. We need to let them hear good news from God where they stand first, before bringing them into our churches.

MISSIONAL LIVING

As the church we must be willing to be immersed in the cultural context of the neighborhood. As missionaries to our cities we have come to declare the relevant reign of the Redeemer—Jesus! As the church, we have come to invade the culture with the gospel and to seek to develop every man, woman, and child to live and walk in light of eternity. We are actively and aggressively seeking to convey God's invisible kingdom made visible. Our outreaches are continual in the neighborhood. We will have cookouts, block parties, health screenings, and coat drives, all with the explicit gospel practiced and proclaimed in front of our neighbors. We pull no punches—we make clear that we are here as Jesus' ambassadors.

We love and are a part of the city. We are here fully aware of the good as well as the bad in our neighborhoods. We are—and gladly want to be—a part of the fabric of the city, and we want the fabric of the city to experience the joy of our King and our God. So we buy dilapidated houses, fix them up, and move in. Dr. Ed Stetzer pounds this point home in his book *Planting Missional Churches* as he states, "Missional means actually doing mission right where you are. Missional means adopting the posture of a missionary, learning and adapting to the culture around you while remaining biblically sound."[28] We adapt and adjust to the community around us. We will get pushed past our comfort and color zone. But in our discomfort we know God is at work. We do life in our community soul-food spots and alongside the cool older man who fixes cars for cheap. I get my candy and chips regularly from the corner store, and the store owner knows me. He speaks Spanish to me, calling me *papito* and I call him *papi*! On the block we say, "We up in here!" As believers we desire to be received by the residents in our city. We want to know our neighbors and we are committed to living amongst them as friends and sons of God.

We understand that rejection is par for the course. But ejection is not an option. We are on a mission to see people we have come to know and love in our neighborhoods have a saving relationship with God through Jesus our Lord. We pray, we preach, we invite, and we cry with our neighbors. We are more than neighbors—we are family. We cry together, hurt together, and laugh together. Jesus has sent us here! Jesus drives my heart and passion for people who do not know Him yet. I am committed to being loved by and loving my neighbors. I am committed to being hated and rejected if that be my lot. I am committed to Jesus and on the cross He has been rejected so that the enemies of God might be called the children of God through repentance in the name of Christ. Jesus is our model! Jesus is our power. Jesus fuels and fires us up to live on the block for the glory of God.

As those engrossed in missional living, we desire cross-centered evangelism to be a virus that crashes Satan's hard drive. We seek to progressively and permanently effect transformative newness and see God's shalom break through the darkness of sin in our city. Yet we are not always happy about the roughness of our community. We visit our friends outside the hood and have temporary reentry issues. Many times we are in this love/hate relationship with the block. But we are here to see Jesus' name be famous. We live out the gospel on the block because we want to lift Jesus' name and draw all men unto Him. This is where we live because mission is our lives. Jesus propels and compels us to stay, soak, and serve on the block.

> **We want to engage the whole person with the whole gospel.**

It is our deep desire to see people embrace missional living. We take the posture of a missionary and become all things to all people so that they may come to know Christ our Lord as their Savior. We want to engage the whole person with the whole gospel, through the means of the whole church reaching out to the whole neighborhood. In order for us to do this we must have a posture and process for maximum effectiveness and long-term impact.

Missional Living Must Be Intentional

The word "intentional" challenges the passivity that can often be the posture of the church as it pertains to the lost people in our cities. I hope that we as a church can learn to be more faithful to hard cities and not run from the neglected lost people out of fear. We must be intentional.

Missionaries are like organic food. We are intentionally grown, watered, and nurtured in specific soil for maximum health. To have the foods that are pesticide free and grown in proper soil requires a great deal of intentionality. So it is in the city that we intentionally go to the least, last, and lost. We must have a plan to connect, care for, and call to our neighbors who don't know Jesus. This will not just happen by spiritual osmosis. We must be intentional; patient but a little pushy. We believe that though God will use the webs of relationships that He has placed into each of our lives, we must sow the Word of God beyond those who are most like us. Jesus calls us to seek the lost with Him. We must intentionally go out and find the good seed, those who have never heard the gospel. We want to see the gospel presented to every man, woman, and child in our townships, center cities, and inner cities.

Missional Living Must Be Developed

Beyond the call from the pulpit for every member of the body to share the gospel, we believe that we must develop sharing with each other. Sharing involves particular days and seasons of outreach when the whole church may serve together, encouraged to show their witness to the neighborhood, or on the mission field elsewhere. This also involves mentoring relationships—where those more gifted and experienced in sharing the gospel encourage those who struggle by actually spending time with each other in their context. We must not assume that people know how to live missionally. We must challenge, teach, and charge each congregant to prioritize this as a lifestyle. We must not just push books at people about the topic of missional living. But we must have classes that train and raise up new leaders from every race and age in our churches to tap into the well of opportunities to lead someone to Christ. We must constantly be about digging into one another's lives through Scripture. Love one another, pray for one another, and confess our faults to one another as we grow and develop for the mission.

Missional Living Must Be Natural

Missional living can only happen if true gospel fruit is growing in our lives. We have to spur each other on to live a life worthy of those around us asking an account for the hope we clearly have. So we long to be a gospel community, not just around those who don't believe, but around each other as we learn to celebrate the gospel of grace daily and grow in all the fruits of the Spirit. As we share the gospel, we develop a natural desire to see those around us taste the mercy we have tasted, even if many things in our lives are not yet as we had hoped. We believe that if we truly drink the water Jesus gives, the eternal spring will well up within us, and our people will never stop sharing the hope they have with others.

Missional Living Must Be Networked

Only as a whole body will we reach the whole community. The idea of the whole body goes beyond the local church's need for every member and their various God-given gifts. Reaching the whole community requires a network of churches that God provides for us to partner with. It's through partnership that we can share resources, people, and a joint vision to see everyone engaged with the gospel. This will call us to work cross-culturally and cross-denominationally. We must open up our missional training to a diverse group, those who are not exactly like us, in order to most effectively reach the lost. One of the most refreshing things about this has been to work with churches that are in a completely different cultural context and denominational tradition than mine. Furthermore, it allows my neighbors to see people of varying ethnic, cultural, age, socioeconomic, and contextual backgrounds working together in my city. It sends the message that not only do I care for them, but that I always invite my friends of all races and places to come to our hood and help build it up. This has been one of my greatest joys—serving in my neighborhood, networked with so many churches that want to see people come to Jesus.

Missional Living Must Always Be Bathed in Prayer

What might take man fifty years to accomplish, God can do in five minutes. Though we take our call to seek and save the lost seriously, we know that a bunch of nervous activity will not be the keys to the kingdom. Everything, even the best-laid and most well-intentioned plans, must be bathed in prayer and given to the one who can work in power. We must not neglect the ministry of prayer and must pray with our families often. We must maintain that God saves through the Savior—not our strategies. We must not develop a strategic arrogance in missional living, but we must remember who is sovereign and at work in and through us. Acts 2 teaches that even though the apostles went from house to house breaking bread, loving and caring for one another, it was the Lord who added to their number daily. Unless the Lord builds the house, they who labor do so in vain. Might we repent of our strategy-dependent living and trust the Lord, pray to Him often, and boldly call to Him to move mightily in our cities.

As we catch a vision for living missionally in any context where the Lord Jesus might place us, I have simply sought to highlight some ways to help us become more effective missionaries. The apostle Paul states in 1 Corinthians 9:24, "Do you not know that in a race all the runners run, but only one gets the prize? Run in such a way as to get the prize" (NIV). Like the apostle Paul we must plan out well and be devoted to missional living as a key to our evangelism and discipleship in our cities. By God's grace we must seek to maximize our missional engagement and create more opportunities to be in and around the people we are seeking to reach with the gospel. I have personally worked to apply these principles and can testify that though they are challenging to our lives, privacy, and family we have seen the awesome effects of God's grace at work through missional living.

In coming to know that community we must emulate the examples set forth in Scripture. We find the greatest example in our Savior, who descended from His position within the Godhead to take on flesh. He came down and became man to *know* our struggles intimately, and so that He might *be known* to us in a fuller way—able as we now are to "behold his glory." We serve a God who can provide for each of our needs because He knows those needs intimately. Indeed, He knows us better than we know ourselves—each and every detail of our existence—down to the number of hairs on our heads.

HOSPITALITY TO THE BLOCK

When a stranger sojourns with you in your land, you shall not do him wrong. You shall treat the stranger who sojourns with you as the native among you, and you shall love him as yourself, for you were strangers in the land of Egypt: I am the LORD your God.

LEVITICUS 19:33–34

When I served as church-plant resident at my home church, Epiphany Fellowship of Philly, I regularly traveled with Dr. Eric Mason to many of his preaching engagements around the country. Somehow or another, on our many trips, I would sit next to, stand in line near, or just use the stall beside a person who would strike up a conversation with me. It was mind-blowing how pure strangers would tell me some of the most intimate details of their lives: divorce, death, adultery, and addiction, to name a few. By God's grace in my two years of traveling with Dr. Mason I saw people come to Christ. Dr. Mason would jokingly say to me "my son in the ministry, Doug Logan, a man who never met a stranger."

My wife, Angel, who serves on the hospitality team at our church, said of me after she saw me having a conversation with a pure stranger one Sunday morning, "Babe, you have the gift of hospitality." I never thought about myself like that. I just thought that that's how it was. I grew up in an African American family and for a few years I lived at my grandfather's house. I had a lot of cousins and friends come, go, move in, move out, and hang out as a regular part of my childhood. Over the years as a pastor in the urban context, I have learned that the heart of hospitality that I had for family members growing up wasn't necessarily the same as the Bible's definition of hospitality.

What does biblical hospitality look like? In Titus 1:8 we see the apostle Paul laying out qualifications for an elder-pastor in Christ's church. Too often these qualifications come with an expectation to simply memorize them for the ordination exam. The apostle Paul wrote this with the intent that Titus and others who would come to be ordained as elders in Crete would live out hospitality, both positionally and actively.

How is Titus's hospitality relevant for the church today? I once read that hospitality means that someone feels at home in your presence. The call to be given to hospitality is an essential part of the continual call to live in active obedience to God by loving and being a friend to strangers. This is one of the keys to missional engagement of the community, along with understanding what it means to be sent, living missionally, and taking responsibility for the lost of the city.

Many evangelical churches simply do not befriend strangers. They suffer from xenophobia where they fear strangers, especially the "stranger within their gates." I know we teach our kids "stranger-danger," and I most certainly taught my kids to scream "stranger-danger" in the event of someone acting suspiciously around them and potentially bringing them harm. However, for us as adults in God's church, God calls us into an intentional life of stranger-danger for the purpose of engaging the stranger and foreigner with the whole gospel. Often churches think they are living out the call to hospitality because they invite their neighbors to their outreaches, coat giveaways, and food drives. However, during day-to-day personal interaction with individual strangers, unknown neighbors and people in need in the community, they are not hospitable. This can create a professional and sterile identity within the community instead of a personal and intimate identity. We need to be believers putting ourselves out there, expecting to meet strangers, and see Christ transform them through our seemingly random but authentic relationships.

Hospitality is a normal exercise in the Old Testament. One example can be seen in Abraham's care for the three strangers who visited him and Sarah in Genesis 18:2–8, 16. Later on we see the way that Laban so graciously extended himself and his home to Abraham's servant in Genesis 24:15–61. Manoah exemplifies a great demonstration of hospitality in Judges 13:15 as he extends kindness toward the angel of the Lord.

Further, we see God specifically charge His people to hospitality through the Levitical law of commitment. Leviticus 19:33–34 states,

> When a stranger sojourns with you in your land, you shall not do him wrong. You shall *treat the stranger who sojourns with you as the native among you,* and you shall love him as yourself, for you were strangers in the land of Egypt: I am the Lord your God. (emphasis added)

Clearly we see that hospitality to strangers was commonly known, encouraged, and expected as a regular practice in the Jewish and Near-East community. The Catholic priest Henri Nouwen says in his book *Reaching Out,*

> Hospitality means primarily the creation of free space where the stranger can enter and become a friend instead of an enemy. Hospitality is not to change people, but to offer them space where change can take place. It is not to bring men and women over to our side, but to offer freedom not disturbed by dividing lines.[29]

Hospitality was originally God's idea, and it is not confined to the history of the Old Testament. All believers today, especially church leaders, are called by God to be hospitable. This is explicitly commanded throughout the New Testament. Romans 12:13b says bluntly "practice hospitality" (NIV). In the passage, Paul is tying both service to the body and care to strangers as a missional command that every Christian must practice in their day-to-day living. Peter instructs that hospitality be offered to strangers in 1 Peter 4:9 by calling Christians to "show hospitality to one another without grumbling." The New Testament, mirroring the Old, is loaded with passages that call and command people to extend kindness to strangers. Here is a short list:

1 Timothy 3:2 (NIV)
Now the overseer is to be above reproach, faithful to his wife, temperate, self-controlled, respectable, hospitable, able to teach.

Romans 12:13
Contribute to the needs of the saints and seek to show hospitality.

Hebrews 6:10 (NIV)
God is not unjust; he will not forget your work and the love you have shown him as you have helped his people and continue to help them.

Hebrews 13:2 (NIV)
Do not forget to show hospitality to strangers, for by so doing some people have shown hospitality to angels without knowing it.

3 John 1:5 (NIV)
Dear friend, you are faithful in what you are doing for the brothers and sisters, even though they are strangers to you.

The leaders in God's church are required to be hospitable or else they are disqualified from ministry. All believers are called to be hospitable. From the factory worker to the executive at the Fortune 500 company, regardless if you have the gift of hospitality or not, you are commanded to walk in friendliness and care toward strangers.

This seems pretty straightforward; what's the big deal? As a pastor in the inner city this seems to be an element of missional engagement that is sometimes missing. On the crime-ridden streets of Detroit, in East St. Louis, Illinois, Newark, New Jersey, and Wilmington, Delaware, the command to hospitality is often modified in the name of "safety!" It is dangerous for my family, and unwise to have strangers in my car, home, and life. Christians ignore

> **All believers are called to be hospitable.**

God's rule for the sake of their own comfort. Followers of Christ excuse themselves with statements like, "Nah, that's not my gifting." These are more than just cop-outs, because according to Scripture they are outright sin!

I've learned in my years of inner-city ministry that hospitality is one of the main arenas to share, show, and saturate the people with the gospel. Contrary to what people may think, people in the hood have closed lives and thick locks on their doors and hearts. As missionaries to the urban streets, friendliness to strangers is one of the key elements to evangelism opportunities. Yes, it's risky! Yes, it could be potentially dangerous. However, we are called to take up our cross and follow Jesus. Jesus went down the street preordained for Him toward death and dying. And with joy and confidence in God, He placed His life in the hands of the God who never lets go of His chosen. The gospel calls us to sacrifice, death, and risk for the sake of Christ, yet always with the promise of the presence of God. Matthew 28:20b says, "And behold, I am with you always, to the end of the age." The writer of Hebrews challenges the church to not neglect the practice of hospitality as he leaves an open idea about missing out on an opportunity to hang out with an angel. As I mentioned before, Hebrews 13:2 (NIV) is a bold reminder to the church in its emphasis on the importance of hospitality to strangers. Angels could be looking for some hospitality!

I have personally been encouraged and blessed by this aspect of my ministry in Camden. I can remember when Angel and I first moved to our block, we took on a full house renovation where we demolished the entire house down to the studs. During the extreme remodeling job of our house, my entire family all chipped in to the completion of the project that took place from April until September of 2011. As a new church planter I was anxious to meet, engage people, see people meet my family, and most importantly introduce them to Jesus as Lord and Savior.

So I told the foreman on the job, Deacon Joe Lanzetti, that he could demolish everything but he must leave us a table, some chairs, and a refrigerator. I did not want to miss any opportunities for missional engagement. I believed that Christ would use the opportunities we had to meet strangers and bring the gospel to bear on their lives. Robert Webber put it this way in referencing the engagement of strangers around meals, "Furthermore, there were no preconditions to eating together. Conversion was no prerequisite to fellowship at a common meal with Jesus. Instead, conversion became a consequence of eating with Jesus."[30]

Because of my desire to see strangers meet the Savior I knew that I needed the table for meals and the refrigerator to store the food I would serve.

I can remember Angel and I inviting nearly twenty-five different people to our house for lunch for meat, chips, and water; occasionally Gatorade. We would work on the house remodeling project with the contractors, and in the process of remodeling we sought to see people's lives reconstructed by the great spiritual makeover contractor, Jesus. We would simply see people walk down the block past our stoop, introduce ourselves, and invite them to lunch.

Questions would be sparked at the table about all types of things. We would converse about interracial marriage all the way to why do churches do things the way they do. From church hurt to relationship advice, I found myself caring for and shepherding many of the people over meals in an empty house with nothing but a table and a refrigerator. Tears were shed in joy and pain at that table. People prayed to receive Jesus at that table. From the people who were shown hospitality in our demolished house, many of them came to meet Jesus as Savior. Again, Robert Webber says, "Today a crucial aspect of evangelism must be that of eating together. It is the primary context for establishing relationships that lead to discussion of things that matter."[31]

This is poignantly true for me in the inner-city communities in which I have served, both Philadelphia and Camden. The meal was so vital for many people as it would be one of the only meals they would eat with a pastor. For me, Angel, and our sons, this was a rich time where Jesus met us in those meals. As Jesus met us in those meals, we as a family fell in love with our block and the city. We learned so much about people and their history as many of the people at the table would tell stories about their lives.

We still laugh and remember Christ meeting us in those conversations at the table on my block in Camden. Most of those people are my good friends today. Muslims and Catholics sat at that table. Pastors and drug dealers sat at that table. God used that table and old raggedy refrigerator as tools and a breeding ground for missional engagement. A table in a demolished house is just one way to practice hospitality. As you are called to practice hospitality in your own unique context, please be prayerful, careful, creative, and wise in your strategies.

CONCLUSION AND CHALLENGE

The physician Luke challenges us with thinking about and living out showing authentic hospitality to strangers. In Luke 14:12–14, the parable of the great banquet, we hear Jesus give us a great treatise on showing hospitality and the biblical view of doing so. Jesus states,

> "When you give a dinner or a banquet, do not invite your friends or your brothers or your relatives or rich neighbors, lest they also invite you in return and you be repaid. But when you give a feast, invite the poor, the crippled, the lame, the blind, and you will be blessed, because they cannot repay you. For you will be repaid at the resurrection of the just."

All throughout His public ministry, Jesus and His disciples were the regular recipients of the hospitality of others, particularly strangers. The disciples regularly went from city to city and town to town without a credit card or a checkbook, depending entirely on the extension of hospitality of strangers (Matt. 10:9–10). Hospitality shown to the early church consisted of the generous hearts of people opening up their lives and their homes. In biblical times this was considered most generous and commendable (Acts 2:44–45).

We can see that this was clearly a regular practice of God's people in both the Old and New Testaments. Further, for God's people to show kindness to strangers was in direct obedience to the Word of God. This reality directly implies that believers can't be on mission while they do not befriend and love people they don't know. You can't talk about being on mission and not talk about having strange people in your house.

The word *hospitality* in Scripture carries the idea of "lover of strangers." So hospitality in the biblical sense was designed for strangers and not just for the people, friends, and family you happen to like. Let us be mindful that this call to show hospitality to strangers does come with a call to discretion and caution in having strangers in your house—you ought not embark here without your eyes wide

> **Living out the call to be a lover of strangers will sometimes invade your privacy and disrupt your comfort.**

open to the risks. Living out the call to be a lover of strangers will sometimes invade your privacy and disrupt your comfort. Yes, as they are in your house and your life, some strangers will absolutely be all up in your business, in your wallet, in your refrigerator, and on your nerves. Living out this call will have strangers from the block in and all over your life. Good! That's mission on the block!

Remember, as strangers are in your life and home, you will have opportunities to see them meet Jesus as Savior. However, remember God is sovereign, not you. There is no promise of conversion or the stranger reciprocating the hospitality. Dr. Daniel Akin in his New Testament commentary on the book of Titus drives this point home, "We are ones who open our hearts and homes to others. In the first-century world, hospitality was a very practical expression of love, not just a source of entertainment."[32]

We are bus drivers in the kingdom of God.

We are vulnerable, exposed, and risking danger to our families and our lives. And yes, they may eat your food and reject you, your gospel, and your God. Yes, they may reject you, hate you, steal from you, and still eat your food on Thanksgiving. However, hospitality is still required even in the worst places. Hospitality is still commanded by God even amongst the lazy, stealing, slow bellies, felons, convicted drug dealers, current and former prostitutes, current and former drug addicts. Hospitality is not a call to be unsafe and naive. But followers of Christ, especially elders and leaders in Christ's church, must not let the fear or lack of clear safety prevent us from obeying God to live out authentic and biblical hospitality.

I call you to be of good cheer. Christians take note, we are bus drivers in the kingdom of God. And many people will get on and off of our missional bus in our lifetime of service to King Jesus. And as they do, we are to be authentically and abundantly hospitable to them all, day in and day out.

Remember, Christian, God has called us to practice, exercise, and show authentic hospitality to strangers on the route of life on which He has sent each of us. Ride on, family of God, remember God is at the wheel. He will use you and your willingness to obey Him through hospitality to the block to reach people with the gospel of Christ. Be encouraged—I testify, it can be done.

PRACTICAL TIPS FROM EXPERIENCE

In Camden, I have tried to spearhead the development in our membership for this sort of engagement. This is always a work in progress, but I thought it might be helpful to the reader to consider a few short practical points that have been helpful in my own ministry.

1. Always Be Discerning about the Tools God Has Provided You

The sovereignty of God must be the first principle of gospel engagement. As a shepherd of a flock, you must be particularly attuned to His purposes for your church. This includes an awareness of the gifts of your members and how best to implement them. You must earnestly review the tools you have been given, and not be afraid to make corrections. If a pastor has a preconceived, preimagined concept of what the music leader should look like, he will be in constant danger of squelching true talent and the Lord's gifting. Similarly, if a pastor has too rigid a preconception of what talents will "work" for his community, then he will ignore the gifts of people who could otherwise have deep impact. Finally, if a pastor is afraid to make changes in leadership positions, then he will not be able to correct the mistakes he has inevitably made.

In our church, our music ministry is ably led by Pastor Trevor

Chin, and we have been blessed with great musical talents from the outset. We have never been in want in this area of our ministry. And yet, God seems to constantly bring us new members with musical abilities. Within the last few years, a classically trained Juilliard violinist came to our congregation. While it might have been a temptation for some to exclude her—either because our music team was "full" or because I felt that classical music wouldn't "reach" the folks of Camden—it was plain to me that her gifts should be used to their fullest extent. She was immediately incorporated into our worship team as well as other musical projects, and the response of our congregation has been overwhelmingly positive!

2. Develop Missional Projects that Are Designed for the Whole Congregation

One way to develop a sense of missional engagement within an entire church is to incorporate the whole church in outreach events. The urban context provides a particularly easy means of doing so, because blocks are used to communal living and large gatherings. Thus, a church picnic or barbecue in a public park or parking lot can easily bring in members of the surrounding community. Thus, the same event can provide both opportunities for fellowship among the church body and for missional engagement.

Such events help foster a sense of communal responsibility within the church for the surrounding neighborhoods. They provide a means for the *whole* congregation to seamlessly involve itself into outreach. Moreover, as members of the church build up relationships within the church body, they start to build relationships with the people in the surrounding community. This in turn helps establish within the whole church body the sort of individualized passion for people and the pressing urgency to see them saved that is crucial for urban missions.

I hasten to add that church leaders must play a crucial role both in organizing such events and fostering a spirit of openness within the church community. They must take the lead in reaching out to surrounding community members, connecting with them on a personal level, and then bringing them into conversation with others in the congregation, undeterred by the awkwardness that sometimes results.

Our church holds barbecues in the summer as part of our First Sunday Fellowship gatherings in our church parking lot. When outsiders inevitably visit, the pastoral staff and I make a point to talk to those people and bring them into the conversation. We have been blessed by the congregational spirit for missions and sense of accountability toward Camden that has developed within our church. As a pastoral team, we are constantly praying for new ways to put our church, as a whole, *into* the surrounding community and vice versa.

3. Develop a Missional "Brand" for the Church

The pastoral team can do a lot to shape a church's identity, and thus it can do a lot to ensure that missional engagement becomes part of that identity. The more boldly the church identity professes its commitment to missions, the more those within the walls will associate the church with those goals. And as members of such a church, they start to understand that this must become part of their identity as well. Thus, "branding" can have a powerful effect on the way in which your congregation participates in missions.

At Epiphany Fellowship, we put missional engagement at

the forefront of our tagline: "On the block, for the city, showing off the glory of Christ." I look for ways to incorporate that motto and identity into my sermons, as those who listen to our podcasts can attest. I feel confident that those who have joined our church understand they are joining a church that seeks to be missionally engaged in its surrounding community. By joining our church, they are implicitly agreeing to participate—at least in some small way—with that mission.

It is my hope that you will join me in reestablishing the church as central to the life of our families and our community. Nowhere in the New Testament is there a commitment to Christ apart from a commitment to the body of Christ, His church. Thus, the call for every person to engage in missional living is a call to every church as well. Indeed, I would go so far as to say that the dynamic of life in a covenant community that flows out to its surrounding, unbelieving community is at the very heart of Christian experience. "The church's mission is to be the presence of the kingdom. . . . The church's mission is to *show the world what it looks like when a community of people lives under the reign of God.*"[33]

WHAT THIS HAS LOOKED LIKE AT EPIPHANY

I believe the best way I can explain what I have in mind is through individual stories of our past experiences at Epiphany. I hasten to add that these are not meant to be prescriptive, but merely descriptive. An "on the block" ministry in Topeka, Kansas, will look very different from an "on the block" ministry in Camden, New Jersey. However, I believe these examples enunciate a certain *heart* and *spirit* that should be common to all forms of missional engagement, no matter its context.

Nu City Bullies—Ministry through Dog Breeding

When I got to Camden in 2011, we knew that some of the most unengaged by the church were Latino and African American fifteen–thirty-one year-olds. As we were speaking with various members of our community, we noticed that a lot of young people in that age group owned or bred a type dog called American Bullies. These dogs are a mix between bulldogs and pit bulls.

Having been breeding dogs for eighteen years, I immediately saw a ministry opportunity. I encouraged others on my pastoral team to get involved, and we started our own breeding under the name "Nu City Bullies." (The name itself was an attempt to communicate gospel truth in the language of the block.)

We have been breeding dogs now for four years. With my schedule being crazy, my dogs have mainly been housed in North Philadelphia with one of our kennel partners. So I took on photography that allowed me access to more breeders all around the region. I really enjoy doing photo shoots for American Bullies as I get to share the gospel all the time with so many people. It has been a wonderful way to meet members of our community, and lead many of them to Christ. Our common interest in dog breeding has provided a starting point of discussion with people who would not ordinarily want to associate with a church pastoral team. One such person was a young man named Kevin. Kevin, as we came to find out, had been a major drug dealer in the city, but he had recently begun breeding bullies. We quickly formed a bond with him through our dogs. Slowly, we were able to discuss spiritual matters and convinced him to come to church. He came to meet Jesus two years later, and I am proud to say that he has turned his life around. His story has become a powerful witness to the gospel and its transformative truth.

E-Spot

We knew of a basketball court near my home that was in desperate need of renovation. Not only was it in poor shape—the concrete was overrun with weeds, and the rims were rusty and bent—the court became a source of cultural and community decay. We came to find out that it had become an easy place for young people on the block to deal drugs—indeed, they could hide behind the weeds.

We determined, in the spirit of Jeremiah 29, that it would be a service to our community to mend this court. We came together as a church and removed the weeds, provided new rims, painted and seal-coated the courts, and renamed it E-Spot. Once we completed the project, we held an open block party to celebrate the new court with our community. We provided food, drink, and a concert with Christian singers. It filled me with joy when people from the community came up to ask us, "Did you buy this?" and "Did the city pay you to do this?" God provided us a powerful opportunity to communicate the wonder of Christ, the glory of His church, and the power of His love. Even the mayor of Camden took note, commending it as an example of the great service of the churches in Camden.

I'm proud to say that the court remains a flourishing gathering place for the community instead of the source of decay it once was.

Book Bag Drive

In the poverty-stricken neighborhoods of Camden, we knew that the start of the school year is often stressful for families. Each year, they must find room in their budget to provide their children with adequate supplies, and very often they cannot. We decided to provide aid to those families by starting a book-bag drive— one in which each child received a book-bag that was filled with new supplies for the school year.

Once again, we made a block party out of it. We set up a moon bounce and had a cookout fully stocked with hundreds of hamburgers. We also were able to partner with local companies to provide some of the children with uniforms, shoes, and sneakers. I even dusted off my old barbershop skills to provide free haircuts. Once again, I was astounded by the outpouring of support we received from our community, but I was overwhelmed by the fact that God had empowered us to image Christ's great power in a broken and dark place.

Morning Manna

Earlier I mentioned that poor nutrition is a major problem in economically struggling neighborhoods, and Camden is no exception. Our church has developed a heart for the children of our area who lack adequate access to healthy foods and thus are set up for a lifelong struggle with their health. Morning Manna was a way for us to combat this unfortunate phenomenon.

On a weekly basis, we set up tables at high-traffic bus stops and some of the bleakest corners in the city. We stand ready with water and healthy snacks for children and their families. We also provide free coffee and breakfast for adults, who are just as malnourished and hungry. Most importantly, we offer spiritual nourishment through prayers and conversations about the gospel.

Although some were wary of our offering at first, Morning Manna has been a blessing to many in our community and has become one of our most rewarding ministries. It is a small gesture that we make, and yet the tangible relief it provides is a powerful display of gospel love that encourages us as much as our community. Many have come to Christ and joined our church as a result of it. Indeed, I have already mentioned one—Jason, the homeless man who was saved a short time before he suddenly passed.

LUCAS

We met Lucas through dog breeding. One of his puppies was sick, and when he saw me he said, "Hey, ain't you a pastor? Help me save this dog. Pray. And hold this one for me." As we were conversing, Lucas wanted to know about my theology since he had grown up in the church—his father was a deacon and later a minister. Lucas had rebelled and stopped speaking with his father. So in addition to talking about dogs and people we both knew, some of our early conversations had to do with theology.

We talked about real life. His girlfriend was white, my wife is white. He was curious to know how I dealt with a white wife, and my wife, Angel, simply told him jokingly, "Just teach her about Jesus, get her some wine and an ottoman and she'll be fine."

I invited him over to the house, he ate with us, hung with us. We talked about dogs and went to dog shows together. He has a house in New York state, so I drove there with him on occasion and began to share the gospel with him. And we became friends.

After several trips to his house in upstate New York, I began to pray and I began to challenge him to get married to honor

God since he was living with his girlfriend and had a baby with her. He asked me if I would officiate and I told him I would. I did marriage counseling with them. Sometime before his wedding, Lucas asked me to come pray for the new house he was buying. When I was there, he just cried; and then he called his father who he hadn't talked to in years and put us all on speakerphone and said, "I want to put you on the phone with my friend; this is Pastor Diddy." Lucas's father asked me, "You a pastor? You're with my son, Lucas?" I said, "Yeah." He just said, "Praise the Lord." He asked, "Do you love Jesus? Do you preach the Bible? Are you married? You're doing the wedding?" When I answered, "Yeah," to all of his questions, he just started exclaiming, "Hallelujah! Hallelujah! Hallelujah!" Lucas got back on the phone with his father and spoke for a long time. God met us in that call.

The wedding was a community affair for Epiphany Camden. I did the ceremony, Pastor T did the music, and his wife, Melissa, sang. Angel helped arrange the flowers, one of our church members DJ'd the reception, and we helped get hotel rooms and everything. In the American Bully dog breeding world, everyone heard about the wedding. It was all over Facebook and it was a pretty big deal. A large majority of Hispanic and African American men in Camden have American Bullies. So my elders and I have American Bullies. And we've seen eleven people come to the Lord based on relationships built through these dogs.

Angel went on to mentor Lucas's wife while I mentored him. We mentored them together. Lucas and his wife are as good a couple as any I've ever counseled because they're both super honest and have the greatest time. My prayer in the middle of all of that has been for them to see the Great Counselor of Jesus over their souls and not just a good counselor in Doug over their marriage. And although they have a heavenward philosophy, I prayed that they would have a redeemed view of the church and the highest view of Christ.

EPILOGUE

I wrote this book to provide guidance on missional engagement, primarily focused on the urban context. I hope and pray that my words will be a service to church leaders and congregations alike. But an important question remains: Are *you* one of those who will be served by it? In other words, are *you* one who has been called to enter the block and be a source of light in great darkness?

I hesitate to use the word *calling* because it is often used as a crutch. Often, we tell others—even ourselves—that "we don't feel called" as a way of hiding the fact that we lack adequate zeal and courage for gospel expansion.

To those who have this disposition, I challenge you to remember the examples of gospel-motivated zeal and courage the Scriptures provide. First, of course, is Christ Himself, who was physically abused from the garden to the grave, and suffered the wrathful condemnation we deserve so that we might have new life. Despite knowing what He was to face, Christ withstood it. He did not call on angels to rescue Him as the Romans plucked out His beard and tore His flesh. Instead He withstood it all, focused solely on bringing glory to the Father and salvation to His people.

Consider also the ministries of His disciples. Just like Christ, these men were met with great derision and physical abuse. And yet they too faced this adversity with incredible steadfastness, incessantly moving forward so that the gospel might spread throughout the whole world.

Finally, consider the exhortations of our church fathers throughout the New Testament, encouraging us to stand strong in the face of danger. Take, for example, the words of Peter, who warns us in 1 Peter 4 to "arm" ourselves (v. 1) and be ready for the world's rejection. We are told "not to be surprised at the fiery trial when it comes" (v. 12), because in so doing we merely "share Christ's sufferings" (v. 13).

I can tell you from experience that you will need courage if you decide to enter the block. For one, it is a dangerous place. The pastoral team in our church has been threatened by violent men, who have flashed concealed guns to demonstrate their seriousness. We have had to break up fights, including some involving knives. Second, urban missions will frequently lead you to the darkest places in the world. Here, Satan has taken hold of people in a manner that can be horrifying and sickening to witness. Abuse, neglect, abortion, prostitution, drug addiction, almost every vile practice imaginable is present in our midst. It takes courage to see such evil, stomach it, and remain hopeful in the gospel and dedicated to its movement.

Do you have that courage? A courage both to enter the block and, when it beats you down, to get up and return to it? It is natural to feel like the answer is no. The sort of courage that makes a believer so singularly focused on the gospel and the glory of God that He is willing to lay down His life for it is supernatural.

Perhaps the better question, then, is are you ready and open to the work of the Holy Spirit to imbue you with that sort of courage and love for the gospel? Would you be willing to join in the words of Nikolaus Ludwig von Zinzendorf (1700–1760), who stated, "I am destined to proclaim the message, unmindful of personal consequences to myself"?

One of the implications of what I have said in previous chapters is that we must find ourselves open to the Lord's will in a revitalized way. Missional engagement is not just an extracurricular pursuit for a certain segment of a church's population. We must see that missional engagement is a core component of the Christian identity. To some degree, we are all called; we are all sent. As George W. Peters put it, "God is a God of missions. He wills missions. He commands missions. He demands missions. He made missions possible through His Son. He made missions actual in sending the Holy Spirit."[34]

If we truly accept these truths about the nature of God and the plan for His people, then the church and its members must be agents of what Roland Allen called the "spontaneous expansion" of the gospel in his book, *The Spontaneous Expansion of the Church: And the Causes That Hinder It*. He describes it as

> the expansion which follows the unexhorted and unorganized activity of individual members of the Church explaining to others the Gospel which they have found for themselves . . . the expansion which follows the irresistible attraction of the Christian Church for men who see its ordered life, and are drawn to it by desire to discover the secret of a life which they instinctively desire to share.[35]

May we not be resigned in our fight to reach the lost because of complacency, frustration, or rejection. May we not be frustrated by failure or succumb to cowardice. May we instead be an intellectual, multiethnic, devil-fighting church, driven to travel anywhere to proclaim Christ's name out of a love for the gospel and a passion for people.

Might we be barrier breaking, aggressive, faithful, fearless evangelists who want Jesus in the hearts and on the lips of all people.

Might our criteria for worship regulate us back to principal points of seeing the lost worship Jesus!

It is my hope that this book be a catalyst for you to hit the street, to hit the road, to hit the block, and share the gospel. There is a block in need of Christ around every corner. Will you go find one?

ACKNOWLEDGMENTS

In ministry and in life we learn from those who come before us. There are many who have invested in my life with their professional mentorship, personal friendship, Christ-like love.

Dr. William (Bill) Krispin, a respected missiologist who took me under his wing and trained me in urban missions. He was the first to teach me the much-needed theological foundations for urban ministry and instilled in me both a passion and a brokenness to serve the people of the inner city.

Dr. Eric Mason poured his life into me by discipling and developing me for church planting. His friendship, love, and faithful ongoing support that he has shown to both me and my family are beyond words of appreciation.

I deeply love my church family at Epiphany Fellowship of Camden. I am more than blessed that Jesus made a way for me to have the privilege of being your pastor. I am grateful that I get to serve a wonderful covenant community in this great and broken city.

To my sons in the ministry: Joe, Ernest, Trevor, A.J., Derrick, Charlie, Dave, and Rich. What a joy it is to serve you. Thank you for serving with me as we seek to be pastors on our blocks, showing off the glory of Christ.

Last, but not least, to Randall, Linda Joy, Adam, Parker and the whole Moody family: thanks for your love, support, work ethic, and long standing commitment to seeing tools developed to advance the cause of Christ in the world.

Special thanks to

Micah Bickford for his editing input and overall harassing phone calls and help. Thanks Bro!

Rob Day for all of his editing help, jokes, and insults. You served me well brother.

And to the Pastor Donny and the Metro Presbyterian Church team, thanks! You went above and beyond for me. Thanks family!

NOTES

1. Crawford Loritts, *Leadership as an Identity: The Four Traits of Those Who Wield Lasting Influence* (Chicago: Moody, 2009), 40.

2. Steven L. Childers, "Church Planting & Development" (handout, Reformed Theological Seminary, Orlando, 1995).

3. Wesley L. Duewel, *Ablaze for God* (Grand Rapids: Francis Asbury Press, 1989), 240.

4. Dean Flemming, "Paul the Contextualizer," in *Local Theology for the Global Church: Principles for an Evangelical Approach to Contextualization* (ed. Matthew Cook et al.; Pasadena, CA: William Carey Library, 2010), 18–19.

5. Chris Hedges, "City of Ruins," *The Nation*, November 2010.

6. Alex Law, "The Untold Tragedy of Camden, NJ," *Huffington Post*, March 8, 2016.

7. Shoshana Guy, "America's 'Invincible' City Brought to Its Knees by Poverty, Violence," NBC News, March 7, 2013.

8. Ibid.

9. Robert L. Plummer, *Paul's Understanding of the Church's Mission* (Eugene, OR: Wipf & Stock, 2006), 124.

10. Childers, *Church Planting Training Manual* .

11. Leslie Newbigin, *The Gospel in a Pluralistic Society* (Grand Rapids: Eerdmans, 1089), 222–23.

12. Christopher J. H. Wright, *The Mission of God's People: A Biblical Theology of the Church's Mission* (Grand Rapids: Zondervan, 2010), 12.

13. Hugh Halter and Matt Smay, *The Gathered and Scattered Church* (Grand Rapids: Zondervan, 2010), 91.

14. Roland Allen, *The Spontaneous Expansion of the Church: And the Causes That Hinder It* (Eugene, OR: Wipf & Stock, 1997), 144.

15. A. W. Tozer, *Of God and Men* (Camp Hill, PA: Christian Publications: 1966; repr. Camp Hill, PA: WingSpread Publishers, 2008), 108.

16. A. W. Tozer, *Man: The Dwelling Place of God* (Camp Hill, PA: Christian Publications, 1966; repr. Camp Hill, PA: WingSpread Publishers, 2008), 182.

17. Darrell L. Guder, ed., *Missional Church: A Vision for the Sending of the Church in North America* (Grand Rapids: Eerdmans, 1998), 6.

18. Thomas Hale, *On Being a Missionary* (Pasadena, CA: William Carey Library Publishers, 2003), 6.

19. JR Woodward, *Creating a Missional Culture: Equipping the Church for the Sake of the World* (Downers Grove, IL: IVP Books, 2012), 27.

20. Jim Peterson and Mike Shamy, *The Insider: Bringing the Kingdom of God into Your Everyday World* (Colorado Springs: NavPress, 2003), 83.

21. Eric Hesse, "What Is Sentness?", Sentness.com, June 7, 2011, https://sentness.com/2011/06/07/wheredoessentnesscomefrom/.

22. Christopher J. H. Wright, *The Mission of God: Unlocking the Bible's Grand Narrative* (Downers Grove, IL: IVP Academic, 2006), 22.

23. Paul G. Heibert, *Understanding Folk Religion* (Grand Rapids: Baker Academic, 2000), 26.

24. Ed Stetzer, *Planting Missional Churches: Your Guide to Starting Churches That Multiply* (Nashville: B&H Academic, 2016), 7.

25. Quoted in *Signs of the Times,* April 1993, 6. Taken from G. K. Chesterton, *Heretics* (1905).

26. Phillip E. Hughes, *Paul's Second Epistle to the Corinthians*, International Commentary on the New Testament (Grand Rapids: Eerdmans, 1962), 210.

27. Heinrich Kasting, *Transforming Mission: Paradigm Shifts in Theology of Mission* (Maryknoll, NY: Orbis Books, 1991); *Die Anfänge der urchristlichen Mission*, trans., David Bosch (Munich: Kaiser, 1969), 127.

28. Ed Stetzer, *Planting Missional Churches* (Nashville: B&H Academic, 2006), 7.

29. Henri Nouwen, *Reaching Out: Three Movements of the Spiritual Life* (Garden City, NY: Doubleday, 1975), 49.

30. Robert Webber, *Ancient-Future Evangelism: Making Your Church a Faith-Forming Community* (Grand Rapids: Baker, 2003), 58.

31. Ibid.

32. Daniel L. Akin, David Platt, and Tony Merida, *Exalting Jesus in 1 & 2 Timothy and Titus* (Christ-Centered Exposition Commentary) (Nashville: B&H Academic, 2013), 238.

33. Robert Webber, *The Younger Evangelicals: Facing the Challenges of the New World* (Grand Rapids: Baker, 2002), 170.

34. George W. Peters, *A Biblical Theology of Missions* (Chicago: Moody Press, 1972), 346.

35. Roland Allen, *The Spontaneous Expansion of the Church: And the Causes That Hinder It* (Cambridge: Lutterworth Press, 2006), 7.

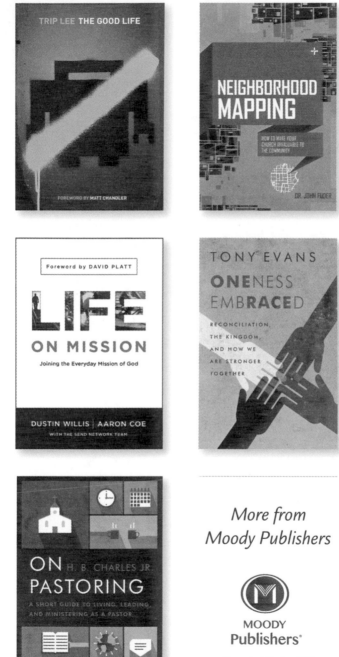

MOODY
Radio™

*From the Word **to Life***

Moody Radio produces and delivers compelling programs filled with biblical insights and creative expressions of faith that help you take the next step in your relationship with Christ.

You can hear Moody Radio on 36 stations and more than 1,500 radio outlets across the U.S. and Canada. Or listen on your smartphone with the Moody Radio app!

www.moodyradio.org